Unleash
THE WORD

Unleash
THE WORD

STUDYING THE BIBLE
IN SMALL GROUPS

KAREN SOOLE

First published in Great Britain in 2015

Reprinted 2016

British Library Cataloguing in Publication Data
A record for this book is available from the British Library

ISBN: 978-1-910587-20-1

Designed & typeset by Pete Barnsley (Creative Hoot)
Printed in Denmark by Nørhaven

10Publishing, a division of 10ofthose.com
Unit C Tomlinson Road, Leyland, Lancashire, PR25 2DY, England

Email: info@10ofthose.com
Website: www.10ofthose.com

Dedication

To Martin, Lizzie, Polly, George and Max

Contents

Acknowledgements

With grateful thanks to all those I have had the privilege of reading the Bible with in small groups over many years. It is a joy to partner with you and to be fed from God's Word together.

Special thanks to all the regional staff teams in UCCF that have helped me sharpen my thinking as I have taught them.

Finally thanks to Martin for his patience, encouragement and support. He has been not only a loving husband but my teacher; without his wisdom I could not have written this.

Introduction

When I was a child my parents and grandparents would juggle babysitting duties between them so that they could go to their midweek Bible study. From my perspective it seemed to be a very solemn and serious thing that they were doing. My grandfather, a French polisher by trade, wore a large stained apron during the day but would change into his suit for the occasion, and my grandmother exchanged her 'pinny' for a hat and gloves. When I joined them in my teens I knew better than to wear my usual attire of jeans and reluctantly put on a pencil skirt. I entered a hall with rows of chairs and quiet, attentive people. The minister preached much as he would do on a Sunday and then several older men prayed long prayers. I sat there as an observer and most definitely not as a participator. When I think back to those days it seems a world away from most expressions of church now.

Today the formality of the old-style midweek Bible study has been overturned and a new freedom discovered. In the last forty years small-group ministry has proliferated in a whole range of expressions. Some meet in churches but others meet in homes, in universities, in workplaces, in coffee shops, in fact anywhere. But it is not the geography or venue that is significant; the biggest change has been the style of leadership. When a church has a small-group ministry, it has members who are small-group leaders; it is no longer one man, the vicar or minister, who teaches every Bible study that happens in the church.

This exciting evolution has enabled many to develop a ministry in their communities as they open up and read the Bible with others. I know of people whose first experience of ministry was teaching small-group Bible study and from that they grew in conviction that they should go into full-time ministry. One London church describes its small-group work as the engine room of their church. These groups bring Christians together to discuss God's Word, learning how to read it well, working out what it means and praying through its implications – all within the umbrella of supportive relationships. Over the years, small-group ministry with unbelievers has also exploded with such courses as Christianity Explored and Alpha becoming nationwide.

Yet this explosion in small groups is not without problems. Some groups try hard to lead Bible studies but veer towards sharing reflections and fail to really get to grips with the Bible passage. In the past the Bible was always taught by a pastor who had been set apart for the task of preaching and studied God's Word with care. I know that there were exceptions to this but in most evangelical churches the handling of God's Word was treated with seriousness. Now there is an attitude that encourages people to 'have a go' and that 'everyone should lead', so people take it in turns to lead their groups. This can be a great opportunity for people to develop their teaching gifts but many lead Bible studies aware that they do not really understand the passage themselves without any help or guidance.

Our world has changed a great deal since the 1970s. We are in the age of new technology: an age where every type of media use *except* reading has increased in the last ten years.[1] Many of us are unused to reading or what I call *really reading*. Consequently we have given up on spending much time reading and meditating on Scripture when we are together. Instead, with a concern to be 'current' or 'relevant', we may construct our meetings around clips from YouTube or become reliant on bought-in courses that can be watched on DVD. Sometimes it seems we have returned to the old model of Bible study that I grew up with – one authority figure telling a group what the Bible says, although now that figure is not the pastor of the local church but international voices from the web. Home-group leaders without strong foundations in the Word are vulnerable in such a set-up. While there is fantastic material available, there are a lot of false doctrines and ideas out there.

We want to achieve so much in our small groups. Lots of churches want them to be missional communities: the small groups in the church provide not only fellowship, Bible teaching and pastoral care but also focus on outreach in the community and evangelism. All these things are very good but (to use an old English idiom) we must not throw the baby out with the bath water. God's Word must remain central in all that we do because it is the foundation of our fellowship, the wisdom for our pastoral care and the message we have to share with others.

I am passionately committed to small-group ministry as a means of building up believers in the knowledge and love of the Lord; supporting and encouraging each other in the gospel; and training us to better handle Scripture. I believe we are at a critical time: a time when we have never had better access to God's Word yet spend less and less time reading it; a time when new expressions of church are growing with enthusiasm and yet within them the gospel message is unproclaimed; a time when young people who have grown up in our churches have no background knowledge of the Old Testament and struggle to articulate what Jesus achieved on the cross.

This book has been written to help anyone who has responsibility for leading a small-group Bible study, whether it is a group for teenagers, students, women, men, old or young. My aim is to give you a vision for your task, to help equip you to read God's Word and finally to give you confidence to lead others in Bible study. I hope this will also encourage you to open up the Bible and read it one-to-one in a variety of settings. I have hesitated in the past to put pen to paper (or fingers to keyboard) because I know the best way to learn to lead Bible studies in groups is at the coalface by doing them. I have made plenty of errors if not every mistake over the years, which has led me to keep on thinking how to do the studies better. But some have asked me if I could put this thinking in a book and so this is an attempt to communicate something that really needs working out in practice. If it leads to others taking the Bible seriously and helps them communicate it to others, I will by God's grace rejoice. Let us recapture serious Bible reading for our generation and listen to His Word.

Should we give up on small-group Bible studies?

What has been your experience of small-group Bible study? Has it been a joy, a time of encouragement, an opportunity to grow in your love and knowledge of the Lord? Perhaps it has been all of those things or none. Maybe some weeks the Bible study has been really good but at other times it has felt as though you were going through the motions. Possibly, if you are honest, the Bible bit of the evening is the weakest part and you go along because you enjoy getting together with other Christians. These relationships are what encourage you – they provide accountability in your Christian life and a sense of responsibility for your church family – whereas the Bible study is like an added extra but not central.

Perhaps you lead a Bible study. Have you ever had a sinking feeling before you set off to lead? Maybe you took the job on because you know it is important and no one else was willing to do it, however now you feel out of your depth and scared every time you begin. Or maybe you work really hard studying a passage before you lead and prepare lots of questions, but when you begin the group look at you blankly and none of your questions work. Or do you feel frustrated by your group? It takes so much effort to prepare for it and yet often group members fail to turn up and don't even let you know they're not coming. You know that Bible truth is life-changing and transforming but no one seems to be excited or challenged or convicted. The Bible study feels like an academic exercise, a duty not a delight. Or perhaps no matter what you do people always drift away from discussing the Bible and end up sharing their own experiences.

Many of us approach group Bible studies with conflicting emotions; we want to study God's Word with others, we know it is important but sometimes the whole exercise feels like ploughing through treacle. The most animated anyone gets all evening is when the discussion turns from the Bible and people begin to talk about football or the latest film they have seen. Each reply to a question is hard won and every answer is brief and followed by a long silence. As a consequence the leader fills in the gaps and talks far too much while gradually becoming aware that everyone else is switching off and looking at their watches. The remarkable thing is that each week folk turn up. They want to come, they do want to meet together and study God's Word but they can't help feeling that they are being short-changed. Is there a way of really engaging with God's Word together so that everyone benefits?

People who have a heart to serve can find themselves given the responsibility of leading a Bible study group but often feel out of their depth in terms of both Bible knowledge and leadership skills. There can be several consequences of this: the leader may be dependent on published material of mixed quality and which does not translate well into their particular setting; the group can begin to lack cohesion and people perhaps become erratic in their attendance; the

6

small group possibly starts to spend most time sharing and praying together, with less and less time engrossed in reading God's Word; eventually the group may focus on alternative activities instead or gradually diminish in size until they decide to give up altogether.

Of course there are many positive experiences of small groups in churches. Some testify to their enormous value: I am one of them. I look back to my student days at St Helen's Bishopsgate when I reluctantly joined a small group to study Mark's gospel. I thought I knew the gospel, after all I had been brought up in a Christian home and became a Christian as a small child, so I confess I was enormously arrogant. I now thank the Lord for those who persevered in encouraging me to join this group because it revolutionised the way I studied the Bible. It not only gave me clarity about who Jesus is and what He came to do but it began my journey in how to understand the Bible. I suppose you could say it taught me how to read. Over the years I have led many Bible study groups in various settings and seen the same thing happen to others. Reading God's Word together reveals God's truth to us while simultaneously teaching us how to understand God's Word better and therefore know Him better.

But some churches are losing confidence in small-group Bible study. There are several reasons for this. Perhaps they are fed up with the frustration of sitting around together in a Bible study that feels like pulling teeth, or perhaps other multi-media presentations seem more dynamic and immediately relevant. In some churches small-group ministry can become quite unhealthy: a place where teaching is not accountable, relationships become cliquey or people fall out. One Christian leader was once reduced to saying, 'Small groups are the worst thing that has happened in the church in the last thirty years.' Church leaders are not routinely taught how to lead Bible studies in theological college and their experience of them may have been poor. Preaching and leading small groups are different skills and small-group ministry may be something they do not naturally feel comfortable with. It is also hard for busy pastors to prepare Bible study material for their home-group leaders to use, therefore the midweek Bible study becomes one more pressure and an extra burden. So perhaps small-group ministry should be avoided? In a strong Bible-teaching church, are Bible study groups an unnecessary extra meeting?

To answer this it is important to consider what small-group Bible ministry adds to the life of a church. By meeting together to read and study the Bible in small groups we are living out the instruction that Paul gave to the Colossians: 'Let the message of Christ dwell among you richly as you teach and admonish one another with all wisdom' (Colossians 3:16).

This injunction was addressed to the whole body of Christ, for everyone to be involved, not just in speaking any encouraging words but also in speaking to one another the message of Christ. Our Bible studies can be a place where we help one another to dwell richly in the Word and begin to teach and admonish one another. They can help us begin to talk about the Bible together and for the Bible to be the natural focus of our conversation. In our churches we want Christ's Word to govern us, but how often do we manage to talk about it even after we have all sat through a sermon? It seems to be amazingly difficult for us to talk about the Bible; instead we find ourselves discussing the sports results, our weekend, our kids, our plans for the week to come, in fact everything but God's Word. Speaking the Word of Christ is not our natural inclination. Even when we have a strong desire to talk about the gospel, we hesitate even among ourselves because we fear we may be seen as 'overly spiritual' or pushy. Yet small-group Bible studies are a place where we can begin to talk together over an open Bible in a safe environment and help one another grow in gospel confidence. Discussing God's Word together not only teaches us to feel comfortable talking about Christ with other believers but can begin to give us boldness to open up a Bible when we are in one-to-one situations, maybe eventually reading and studying the Bible with a non-Christian friend.

The best small groups complement the life of a church by adding something that Sunday services alone cannot provide. In the sermon the preacher speaks into a large group. He has prayerfully prepared, not only seeking to understand the text but also working out how to communicate it and apply it in the most appropriate way. God speaks through this proclaimed Word and the Spirit applies it to our hearts and minds. Even though we struggle to discuss the sermon afterwards, we know that God's Spirit works in every hearer's life, convicting them of the truth of the Word and transforming individuals to become more like Christ. The preacher rarely gets instant feedback (although some address this by building in a question time or even receiving tweets during the talk) but it is generally fair to say the sermon is a process that involves one man communicating to many in a kind of scattergun approach. He hopes to faithfully teach the truth in a way that will relate to those he is teaching but is aware that he may not be able to engage everyone. However, the group study is an interactive process which brings the opportunity of engaging directly with individuals. It is hard to fall asleep in a small group and not be noticed! (Actually when my husband was a junior doctor he did fall asleep but the group in kindness only woke him up if he snored too loudly.)

The dynamic nature of group Bible study is its strength; God's Word is being taught in a relational way. The preacher may guess that hearers will find a particular verse difficult and seek to address it; in a Bible study these difficulties will be made explicit and it may turn out that people have difficulties and questions that you have never thought of. As a study develops it can become clear that people are further on in their understanding or further back than you had imagined. The Bible study leader has to be responsive and think on their feet in a way that the preacher does not. It is this element of small-group work that is at once thrilling and daunting. This is the truly scary bit of small-group ministry; you have no idea what others are going to say!

As a leader this can make you feel very vulnerable. For example, in one of my studies someone once started speaking authoritatively about the original Greek of the passage and it turned out that he had studied ancient Greek at Cambridge. However, this proved to be of great value to us all, although it was a little intimidating to begin with! We worry that we do not know enough, and that we will not be able to answer people's questions. We worry that we will not be able to manage a discussion, or that people will disagree, or that they won't say anything. In short we worry that we will fail both in our understanding of the Bible and in our ability to lead a discussion around it. But we can turn this fear on its head because the very thing we find difficult – the response of others – is the strength of a small group.

A small-group leader is not there to lecture group members, but to help them engage with the text. Through this engagement individuals can see if their understanding fits with what the passage says. In a study wrong thinking about the Bible can be exposed in a way that provides an opportunity for the leader to help people move on in their understanding. In a small group where individuals know and trust one another, we can help each other become more in line with God's Word. Sometimes we will discover that we thought that the Bible said something that it doesn't; at other times we will be discovering things that are completely new to us. Reading the Bible like this together in a group should sharpen everyone. The key element for the leader in this process is knowing what questions we need to ask of a passage in order to help one another read it.

Paul urged Timothy to: 'Do your best to present yourself to God as one approved, a worker who does not need to be ashamed and who correctly handles the word of truth' (2 Timothy 2:15). This is a valuable injunction for the Bible study leader. Our task is to correctly handle the Word of truth. Bible handling is a skill that we improve on even as we lead our studies week after week. As we ask questions of a passage we model to our groups how to handle the Bible better.

One of my greatest joys as a leader has been when people in my group grapple with the text, and ask challenging questions of me. It gives us all an opportunity to check out if we are handling the Bible correctly. I confess that in the middle of a study when someone challenges something I have said, it can initially knock me off guard, but after a few moments of reflection I am really grateful as it teaches me too. It is vital at this point to acknowledge what has happened: 'Yes, I am wrong – that point is really helpful. Does everyone else see this?' So rather than questions being something to fear, I rejoice because they are part of what it means for us to be just like the Bereans: 'Now the Berean Jews were of more noble character than those in Thessalonica, for they received the message with great eagerness and examined the Scriptures every day to see if what Paul said was true' (Acts 17:11). Asking questions and checking

11

what the Bible says is something that we should encourage. The real tragedy is when people show no appetite to really understand God's Word, not when people carefully keep checking everything.

At heart the task of a leader is to help others discover what God's Word says. A small-group Bible study can help us *really* read the Bible instead of just assuming we know what it says. When this is done well, the Bible study becomes a place that involves everyone in changed understanding to changed thinking and living. I am convinced that small-group ministry is a brilliant way to engage with others over God's Word, and these principles of small-group ministry are transferable to a variety of other settings – from youth groups to investigating Christianity groups as well as for groups of mature believers meeting together to build one another up in their faith and even in one-to-one ministry.

So as we approach the idea of leading a Bible study, we have two aims in our minds: the first is to get people to really engage with God's Word so that they are rooted in Christ; the second is to make sure the Bible is handled well within a context that handles people well. The model of Bible study that this book will seek to outline is based on these two principles: we need to read God's Word well and listen to others motivated by our love of God and our love for those in our group.

I hope that by the time you have finished this book you will have greater confidence that leading Bible studies in groups and reading it with individuals is something that you can do. For now it is important to underline the fact the Bible study leader does not need to *know* everything but does need to model a desire to sit under the authority of God's Word, a hunger to learn and a heart for others.

Is there a `right answer`?

The room is full and there is a warm buzz of conversation, drinks are sipped and a rather delicious cake is passed around. The Bible study begins and the group settles down with an expectant hush. Someone opens in prayer and the passage is read. What follows resembles a game of tennis. A question is served by the leader and hit back by a group member. The leader asks another question and someone else responds. The questions are directive and the rallies short. During this exchange many of the group are merely spectators; the warm buzz of the earlier chat has vanished. It is clear that the leader has an answer in mind when they ask their question. Some group members never speak because they are afraid that they will get the answer wrong. The group becomes progressively quieter as the study continues and finishes when the leader tells everyone what the passage is about.

In a different church another small group meets. There is the familiar chat before the study begins. This study begins with prayer as well. The passage is read and then the leader asks an open question: 'What do you all think?' There is an explosion of voices as various people have been reminded of something they heard somewhere before and are keen to share their stories. Others are familiar with this passage and immediately share how it has impacted their lives. Another voice pipes up with the words: 'I like to think …' This is followed by a completely contradictory idea by another person who says: 'Well, to me …' Finally the group leader draws it all to a close with a prayer when they realise what the time is.

Are either of those scenarios familiar? I have experienced both. Different churches have different tendencies. Some run Bible studies that make you feel as though you were in school; their studies are rigid with little room for discussion, though their strength is that the leaders have a strong commitment to the Bible and proclaim its truth. Other churches see the small group as a chance to develop relationships and a place to encourage one another; their Bible study is a springboard for people to share with each other things that they already know and their strength can be in the relationships that develop. So both approaches have strengths: it is good for people to learn truth when they come to Bible study and it is good for people to engage with each other over God's Word. However, the first model denies a group the opportunity to engage with the text relationally so that in some instances they might as well give up the pretence of it being a group Bible study and listen to a talk instead. The second approach fails to help the group move on in their understanding, instead becoming a place where people discuss their experiences and what they already know. Both approaches can be frustrating if you want to grapple with what God is saying and grow in your own knowledge and love of God.

In reality a lot of group Bible studies move between both approaches, at times very directive and other times much looser.

Underlying all of this is our approach to hermeneutics. Hermeneutics is an intimidating word to describe the art or science of interpretation, or for our purposes how we interpret the Bible. Using a term like hermeneutics may make you want to skip this chapter but I ask you to bear with me because if we can understand how hermeneutics fits with small-group Bible study, we will be able to address both of the previous scenarios.

I show my age by admitting that I remember when 'I Don't Like Mondays' by the Boomtown Rats was the UK number one. Now I'm going to ask you, reader, to try to remember it as well, and if you have never heard it, check it out on YouTube (do it now before you read on). What is this song about? The title gives you some clues! I have played this song to folk of various ages, from students to those who are now retired, and asked them the same questions: 'Well, what do you think? What is this song about?' Here are a selection of the different responses I have had:

→ 'It's about not liking Mondays.'
→ 'It's about a teenager who doesn't like school especially on a Monday.'
→ 'It's about the universal feeling of being stuck in the rat race that is symbolised by the Monday morning feeling.'
→ 'It's saying something about new technology – robot feelings, and a silicone chip inside a head.'
→ 'It's about parents trying to understand their teenager.'
→ 'It's about a school shooting that was justified by a teenage girl with the words: "I don't like Mondays."'

The last answer is right but it is only given by those who have heard the context of the song before. Bob Geldof wrote it after hearing the news of a shooting at Grover Cleveland Elementary School in San Diego, California in 1979. Brenda Spencer killed two adults and injured eight children. When asked why she had done it, she replied: 'I don't like Mondays.' Once you know that fact you can never hear the song in the same way again. All of the other answers that people gave were derived from the lyrics as they tried to make sense of the song. Different parts of the song resonated with different people, hence the variety of meanings. Some struggled to make out all of the words and could only glean a small part of what the song was about (Bob Geldof is not renowned for his clear diction), while others had prior knowledge that changed the way they heard the song. This exercise of interpretation is an exercise in hermeneutics. This act of interpretation is what we do whenever we read a Bible passage.

In the past, ideas of how we understand texts were quite simple: we believed that it was a matter of developing a few rules, applying them and then the answer would become clear. Everyone accepted that the author had an intention in writing and that it could be clearly communicated and understood. In a Bible study this seems particularly pertinent. God has given us His Word and His Word has a meaning that we discover by reading it and asking the right questions. This traditional approach involves the reader asking interpretive questions of a text so that it can be understood as the author intended.

But many people nowadays doubt whether this clear understanding of the text can be achieved. In fact some postmodern scholars insist that it is impossible to read an absolute objective meaning in a text. After all, in my experiment with the song most listeners failed to understand the ideas that Bob Geldof was trying to express. Can we go as far as saying that those who felt the song was about the 'Monday morning feeling' heard that idea because they themselves experience the 'Monday morning feeling', and those who believed it was about the dangers of new technology were alert to that idea because they are concerned about the impact of new technology in the modern world, and those who tuned into the line about 'Daddy' were the parents of teenagers? The problem is that we can never approach anything completely objectively; we come with our own baggage, our own insights, our own experiences and our own issues.

For the postmodern reader this is the joy of the process. As a text is read it is experienced in a unique way by each reader, enabling them to encounter not an outside truth but a revelation of self. As Roland Barthes writes: 'Whenever I attempt to "analyse" a text which has given me pleasure, it is not my "subjectivity" I encounter but my "individuality", the given which makes my body separate from other bodies and appropriates its suffering or its pleasure: it is my body of bliss I encounter.'[2]

In its crudest form reading becomes a discovery about myself rather than a truth outside of myself. Human consciousness becomes the source of reality, so what the reader understands and encounters cannot be wrong. It exalts individuality over revealed truth. The effect of this on our Bible studies is twofold: first it has resulted in a proliferation of experience-based, human-centred Bible studies; and second, during a Bible study everyone can have a different take on the passage with all views and opinions being seen as equally valid. It means that we approach a Bible study with an attitude that is seeking to discover truth about ourselves rather than truth about God. It is a long way from the traditional Bible study approach.

By now I imagine all sorts of alarm bells may be ringing with you – this postmodern approach to reading the Bible sounds dangerous. It is tempting to reject this form of thinking altogether, yet if we do that we will be ignoring an insight that the postmodern scholars helpfully brought. Readers do interpret texts differently. Readers cannot read the Bible without already having some kind of framework that impacts the way the text is received.

I was once in a church when 1 Corinthians 14:34–35 was read out loud by a woman who found it such an alien idea that she giggled as she read it. Her mindset was: 'This Scripture cannot be taken seriously because women have equality and that means there is no difference in our roles.' She had a view of Scripture that meant that although its meaning seemed clear, it must in actuality mean something different for us today and therefore we are free to laugh at the archaic view that Paul was advocating. If she were reading this passage in a Bible study group it would be as though she were wearing 'feminist' glasses as she did so. The leader's job would be to help her read the passage without her glasses on, so that she could begin to understand what this passage is really saying and allow her mindset to be shaped by God's Word.

Everyone in a group will have a different perspective; they will be wearing different 'glasses'. Some will have a large body of knowledge built up over years. When they read the passage they may come to a quick understanding or they may assume they know what it says already, because rather than read it with fresh eyes they just fit it into their Bible framework (systematic theology). Sometimes for these Christians, reading the Bible is about spotting truths they agree with but they fail to see other things which are new to them that they do not know. Others in the group may have no biblical knowledge at all and every time they approach a passage it is all very alien. I love the combination of these two types in a group because both have so much to offer the other. The Christian who has knowledge can share it with the one who doesn't, but the one who has little knowledge can bring an unrestrained freshness because they read it at face value and don't sieve everything through their systematic grid first. Bible study groups are a rich mixture of people with their own experiences and perspectives, and the joy of small-group study is that together we can sharpen each other's understanding so we get to grips with what God is actually saying rather than impose our perspectives on it.

But what about the suggestion that it is not possible to ever truly understand what an author was trying to convey (authorial intent)? If this is the case, however hard we try in a Bible study we will never get to a right understanding. This thought sits uncomfortably with us because we know God has revealed Himself in Scripture, but we need to accept in all humility that none of us know all that there is to know about God; if we did we would be God. This does not mean that we cannot understand anything just because we cannot know everything. All of us are on a continual journey learning more and more of God. There is truth to be discovered in Scripture and we need to help each other read it. I believe small-group Bible study can be a brilliant place to do this.

We can help each other to overcome our natural biases that stop us *really* reading the Bible. The Nobel Prize winner Daniel Kahneman,[3] in his book *Thinking, Fast and Slow*, describes two main processes that we use when it comes to decision-making. The first is 'System 1' which is our automatic system of thought – the ideas that come to our heads before we have even consciously begun to think. The second, 'System 2', is a more effortful system – the sort of thinking we have to slow down to do, such as when we calculate a maths problem. Why is this significant in a Bible study? Because when we first read a passage, whether we realise it or not, we will have an automatic response to it. This first response reflects our starting position. If we have been reading the Bible for years and God's Word is deeply engrained in us, our first response might be quite accurate. Alternatively our initial reading might be a long way from the truth of the passage. The group Bible study is an exercise in 'System 2' thinking; a way for us to help each other engage with the text in a more thoughtful way. It is a type of 'slow thinking' that helps challenge our 'System 1' assumptions.

If you have yet to be convinced, perhaps an experiment from the world of psychology will help. Christopher Chabris and Daniel Simons conducted a now famous experiment called 'The Invisible Gorilla'. In this experiment participants were asked to watch a short film and count the number of times a team of basketball players made passes. While concentrating on counting the passes, most participants failed to notice a person dressed in a gorilla outfit walk across the field of play. I have shown such films to many groups and most people watching the clip for the first time do not spot the gorilla. There are variations of this experiment now available on YouTube, including one that not only uses the gorilla but also changes the colour of the curtain at the background halfway through and has a player walk off; those expecting to see the gorilla fail to notice the other changes. The video concludes with the statement: 'When you are looking for a gorilla, you often miss other unexpected events.'[4] Similarly we might think we understand the Bible but often we approach it looking for what we expect to find there instead of coming with fresh eyes. We need each other's eyes to help us overcome our blindness. As Daniel Kahneman says about the general human condition: 'We can be blind to the obvious, and we are also blind to our blindness.'[5] The Bible often describes us in this way; we are all blind until the Spirit opens our eyes. The good news is that God has given us both one another and the Holy Spirit to help us in our understanding.

Don Carson describes our journey into the truth of God's Word with two helpful images. The first is a challenge to the postmodern scholars' belief that we cannot understand a text and rather find ourselves in a hermeneutical circle, going round and round but never able to find truth. Carson describes this instead as a spiral in which we start to spiral into the text: 'Does the hermeneutical circle always have the same radius? Would it not be truer to our experience to say that the radius of the circle gets a little shorter with time – i.e., that we start to spiral into the text?'[6] I have found this idea immensely useful when faced with a group in a Bible study. Imagine a spiral with the centre being the heart of a passage, the truth of God's Word in all its fullness. Everyone who reads that passage will relate to it in some way. Some will be a long way from the centre, others will be closer, but no one will be at the centre (not even the Bible study leader). The aim in a study is for the leader to help everyone move on in their understanding, to spiral deeper into the text, to get closer to the heart of God's Word. Not everyone will necessarily arrive at the same point by the end of a study, but the aim is for everyone to move closer to the centre from where they started.

If you are thinking that it is not fair to say we will never get to the centre of the circle, Carson explains further with a second illustration, this time from the world of mathematics. I am not a mathematician so I take the truth of this on trust. It is based on Karl Popper's asymptotic graph: 'An asymptote is a curved line that gets closer and closer to a straight line without ever touching it.'[7] In practice these two lines can get so close that the naked eye may think they are touching but in fact they never will. Our understanding of God is like this; we will never fully know Him because we are not yet face to face and we will never be God! So meaning and truth do reside in the Bible text but we are fallen creatures who only see in part now: 'For now we see only a reflection as in a mirror; then we shall see face to face. Now I know in part; then I shall know fully, even as I am fully known' (1 Corinthians 13:12).

We will always be limited in our understanding of God because we are living in a fallen world and do not yet see God face to face. Learning the gospel is a gradual process, but the smallest child who believes it is saved by faith. The wisdom of God is in the gospel: It is simple yet immense; possible for a child to believe but beyond our understanding. The gospel saves us and the gospel sustains us. We never grow out of it, we never grow beyond it but as we read the Word we will gain deeper insights into the simple truths that we first heard and discover the profundities and depths of God's purposes. As we read His Word we grow in our knowledge of Him and we will never exhaust it. What a joy to know that all of us from the youngest believer to the most mature saint can keep reading and studying the Bible and continually spiral deeper and deeper into God's truth; we can get closer and closer on the asymptotic graph to the axis of God's truth but we cannot ever exhaust the Bible so that we have nothing left to learn. What a joy to know that every time I read God's Word there is more to learn, more to meditate on, more depths to plunge. It is as though we are spiralling into deeper treasures and more profound truths.

We began this chapter by looking at two types of Bible studies: one represents the modernist approach but it neglects people and relationship, and it ignores the fact that everyone in the group starts with a unique position in relation to the passage being studied; the other represents the postmodern approach – it allows group members to express their positions and encourages their unique relationship with the text, but fails to help them move on from their current understanding by helping them engage with the truth of the text.

A small-group Bible study can be the place where the weaknesses of both are overcome. By reading the Bible together it is possible to help each other identify the things we miss when we read it using our own personal framework. It can help us to sharpen our understanding and move closer to God's revealed truth. We are all continually learning together. We will never 'crack' the passage as though we are breaking a code, although there will be occasions when there are great breakthroughs in our understanding. Sometimes in a study one person will move a long way in their understanding but others will seem to hardly move at all. The aim of Bible study is not necessarily to get everyone to give the 'right answer' or arrive at the same place, but it is to help everyone – whether they begin with a good understanding or are a long way off – move closer to the truth of God's revealed Word.

Reading the Bible together in small groups is an exercise in hermeneutics but it is also much more than that because the Bible is so much more than any other work of literature. It is God's inspired, 'breathed out' Word to us. Our studies can help us reflect on the

Bible together, to read what it is saying, but God is at work divinely too to give us insight. When His Word is read, He is present teaching us, the Spirit will convict us and He helps us each individually in our relationship with Him. There is a lot more to say about this but that is for another chapter.

Approaching God's Word

Leading a Bible study can be a lonely business. It is ironic that although leading a small group is all about relating with people, it involves spending a lot of time on your own to prepare. This can be hard for those of us who enjoy being with people but struggle to discipline ourselves to study, yet there is no escaping the fact that if you are going to lead a Bible study you need to be prepared. On the other hand those of us who enjoy time alone quietly studying God's Word can find the most daunting part about leading a group being the interaction with others. We all have different strengths and weaknesses; the introverts among us thrive in front of an open Bible at their desk but not in front of a group with open Bibles on their laps; the extroverts struggle at their desks but become energised when meeting with others. Yet whatever our temperaments we need to keep hold of two principles: we need to first *really know and rejoice in God's Word*, and second r*eally know and love God's people*. Regardless of our particular weaknesses or strengths we need to keep on developing in *both* of these areas. I am certain that both introverts and extroverts make great leaders if they have a love of God, His Word and His people; if we have a heart for God and love His Word we will have a desire for others to know God's Word; if we have a heart for others we will long to see them grow in their love and knowledge of God by feeding from His Word. Having this heart will cause us to continue to spiral into the Scriptures, plunging into God's truth, so we will know God better ourselves and be able to serve the others in our group.

Leading a Bible study group is more than just facilitating a discussion. It is rare for a group to get further on in their understanding of a passage than the group leader has themself. Alternatively if we don't understand it, we risk passing our confusion on to others. That is not to say that we will ever completely master a text – sometimes we have to lead passages aware that we do not comprehend them as well as we would like. But it is crucial that as leaders we take responsibility to seek to understand a text in order to lead others into a deeper understanding of it themselves. It will mean sacrificing time in a busy schedule; it will mean finding time by getting up early at the weekend or staying up late in the evening, finding a quiet half an hour during a lunch break or giving up an evening in front of the TV. We will have to set time aside to read and meditate on God's Word. It is a central yet lonely and unobserved part of a leader's role. It can be tough but it pays dividends when faced with leading a group. Take encouragement from Paul's letter to the Colossians: 'He is the one we proclaim, admonishing and teaching everyone with all wisdom, so that we may present everyone fully mature in Christ. To this end I strenuously contend with all the energy Christ so powerfully works in me' (Colossians 1: 28–29).

Paul's desire was to build up others so that they would stand at the last day 'fully mature' before Christ's throne. This is our ministry too, whether we are teaching those who are not yet Christian or those who are mature believers. Such ministry is hard work but we are not doing it alone. The miracle of Christian service is this: as we labour, *Christ's* energy works in us! It is His work too! So while we will find leading Bible studies hard and at times exhausting, remember Christ works in us and through us as we serve faithfully to build up others.

So where do we start when we have a passage to teach? How do we study the Bible in order to faithfully prepare it to help others? There are many excellent books that have been written that address this question in detail, some of which are listed at the end of this chapter. For now here are a few foundational principles.

Pray!

Prayer needs to be at the heart of what we are doing. We pray that God will give us understanding as we approach His Word, that He will help us study it and that He will speak to us as we meditate on it. We ask Him to teach us and nourish us before we teach it to others. It is very easy to view preparing a study as a job to be done, and find ourselves not even reading the passage properly before trying to put questions together for the group that we are leading. But when we do not listen to God or allow His Word to impact our lives before we seek to teach it to others, we fall into the trap of making Bible study an academic exercise, legalistic and cold, displaying nothing but our own hypocrisy. God's Word is living and breathing, not just a series of ideas to be spotted. Reading the Bible is not like reading any other literature; we read the Bible in relationship with the author, an on-going and developing relationship.

Prayer is central to this.

Such is my weakness that sometimes I need to pray just to get started. I am easily distracted; it only takes an email in my inbox or a click on to Facebook and time drips away. I pray frequently for self-discipline!

Finally pray that our preparation will be fruitful and used by God to equip and build up others despite our frailties and failings!

Read

This is the most fundamental and obvious thing to say but the more I lead Bible studies, and sadly listen to some sermons, I have realised that this is a hard thing to do. We have considered already that our framework can blind us to ideas that may be in a passage: we need to do everything we can to come to a passage fresh and not assume we know what it is saying already. But I think we have another problem that has increased as our use of technology has increased – we are generally poor readers. We can read but we fail to give anything our attention for very long. We have learnt to skim-read and scan material, rarely pausing to linger and take a longer look.

Jakob Nielson researched the eye patterns of readers while they were using the web and a very clear 'F'-shape pattern emerged. Readers would read the first sentence or two and then scan down, picking up a little material from the second paragraph and then sweeping to the bottom. If you are reading this book perhaps you are avoiding this approach but I often skim-read in this way. There is value in speed reading in a world that overloads us with material but the exception to this must be the Bible. When we read Scripture we need to savour every word. If we are to '*really* read' we need to slow down. As T. David Gordon explains: 'Reading texts demands a very close and intentional reading.'[8]

Friedrich Nietzsche first used the term 'slow reading' way back in 1887. He asserted that it was essential when reading to go aside, to take time and to become still.[9] This is what we need to do every time we seek to study the Bible. We should read a section over and over again. As we do this we will begin to identify the flow of a passage and then we can return and look at the details. *Really* reading will mean that we will stop and meditate on the way a sentence is formed, the words that are used and how the sentences fit together, and we will contemplate why it has been written in that way. Reading slowly is not our natural gear but, as John Miedema points out, if we do it not only will our comprehension increase but we will discover gems.[10]

Lancelot R. Fletcher, a philology professor, described how he encouraged his students to learn the skill of slow reading by asking them to imagine that the text they were reading was written by God:

'The purpose of asking you to assume that the text for the course is written by God is to give you the opportunity to learn.'

'How so?'

'Well, if you are going to learn, and you are going to learn from the author of this text, then I suppose there must be something you have to learn from that author. Right?'

'I suppose so.'

'And what you have to learn from the author (in this case Plato) must then be something about which you know less than the author.

It might even be something about which you have incorrect opinions or assumptions. Do you agree?'

'Yes.'

'Now, when you read a passage in a book and you find the passage unclear or inconsistent with what you already think, do you immediately say to yourself, "Here is an opportunity for me to learn"?'[11]

When we are reading the Bible we don't have to imagine the author is God because we are reading *His* words! This amazing truth in and of itself compels us to slow down and gives us cause to pause. When we find things that seem hard it is an opportunity to learn, but more than that it is an opportunity for us to grow deeper in our relationship with God.

Reading a passage aloud is very helpful because its very nature forces us to slow down and make decisions about meaning through intonations. Often when we read aloud we notice that we have placed the emphasis in the wrong place; this is because reading aloud engages our sense of hearing and helps us identify patterns, the flow of the passage and repeated words and ideas, and it can also help us hear where the punchline is. The Bible was written to be read aloud to its original recipients who did not have the advantage of the printing press or for many even the ability to read. The Bible is beautifully written so that hearing the words gives us a deep sense of their meaning.

↳ Translations

Really reading a passage can take us a long way forward in our understanding but the Bible was written in a different language and we must respect the fact that we are reading a translation before we place too much emphasis on English words. I am no language scholar but others are and the good news is that there are some excellent modern versions whose translators have strived to convey the original meaning as closely as possible. Because of this I find it useful to read a passage in more than one version. I use the ESV and NIV in preference but increasingly I check out the Holman Christian Standard Bible too. Sometimes I teach groups that come with a variety of versions and so I will read these in my preparation. This is easily done online, for example with http://www.biblegateway.com.

Commentaries are also helpful in addressing language issues. These can be very expensive, however the second-hand market is easy to access online. If you try to get a reliable commentary every time you spend a length of time in a Bible book, over the years you will build up quite a library.[12]

A good rule of thumb when studying Scripture in translation is to be very careful before drawing major conclusions based on the use of one particular Bible word in one particular version. Try instead to work out which fits best with the context of the passage and then check out what others have taught in the past; generally commentaries will clarify important issues.

Contexts

There are several contexts that we need to consider: historical; geographical; literary; and biblical – where a particular passage fits into biblical salvation history.

⌐→ Historical

The Bible is a collection of ancient texts, written into a

particular time, place and culture. The world the Bible describes can be alien to us, so some historical background can enable us to appreciate what is going on. For example, when reading the gospels it is useful to understand why tax collectors were so despised, or who the Samaritans were, or the difference between the Pharisees and the Sadducees. In fact there are many details that needed no explanation to the original readers but are unfamiliar to us today. This is where commentaries, or a Bible dictionary, come into their own.

But I want to add a word of caution; God has given us His Word and it is sufficient. Often we will get the gist of a passage purely by reading it well, so we must take care not to conclude something from a passage that its original hearers would not have done. Some people use the historical argument to teach things that the Bible does not teach – this is particularly the case when it comes to interpreting the contentious passages concerning women's ministry. We must not use history to undermine principles that the Bible still teaches. Rather the historical context can help us understand what the original recipients of God's Word understood when they first heard the Word preached to them and the revelation of God that they received is still the one we need to see too. As Dick Lucas, the former Rector of St Helen's Bishopsgate, said, 'God's Word to them then will be God's Word to us now.'

↳ Geographical

I confess to being a poor map-reader, thus taking my family on some very unfortunate detours. Geography in the Bible can also take us on long detours, looking at maps and getting nowhere!

As a child I coloured in maps in Sunday school classes with no understanding at all. But though it has taken me a long time, finally I have come to appreciate that when it comes to the Bible geography matters and place names are important. Sometimes checking these out will reap great benefit. For example, Gerasenes (Mark 5:1) reveals that Jesus went to Gentiles as well as Jews. My personal favourite place name is found in Hosea 2:15: 'the Valley of Achor' that God promises will become 'a door of hope'. Where is the Valley of Achor? It is the place where Achan and his family were stoned in Joshua 7:24–26. This was a place of 'trouble', of judgement and wrath, yet God promises in Hosea to turn it into a place of hope. Meditating on this truth is incredible: a place that had been known as the valley of trouble is transformed, becoming instead a place where wrath is turned aside, a hope that is ultimately fulfilled in the cross. Not all place names reap such great reward when looked up but it is a worthwhile part of our preparation that at times explodes our understanding.

↳ Literary

When reading the Bible it is vital that we remember that it is an amazing library of books written in a wide variety of styles from poetry, history and narrative to apocalyptic. To understand any given passage we need to appreciate its form and read it accordingly. As we grasp the imagery, the metaphors and the truths that these forms contain, we will be able to delight more and more in the Lord. Kathleen Nielson writes: 'Reading the Bible for more than propositions means that we relish its beauty more and more, as that very beauty leads us more fully to grasp its truth.'[13]

⮑ Biblical

When I was a teenager my Bible-reading habits were terrible, not because I struggled to read it (although I often did) but because I treated the Bible as a magic book that could be opened at random to get a *word* for the day. I was very good at imaginative interpretations from Old Testament passages in particular. My Bible seemed to have the habit of opening up in Joshua, particularly at passages about serving and fighting before receiving an inheritance, which I managed to interpret as 'serve God faithfully now and you will get married'. You can imagine this form of Bible reading left me dangerously vulnerable and I nearly rejected the gospel altogether.

I cannot emphasise enough how important the context question is. So much of our misunderstanding and false teaching comes from failing to read the text in the context in which it was written. I do not know who first said it but it remains true: 'A text without a context is a pretext for a prooftext.' If we take a verse straight off the page and ignore its setting we can make the Bible say almost anything – for example, it is possible to take verses from Romans (such as Romans 2:7) and teach that we are all saved by good works, which is the complete opposite of Paul's argument. We would never read any other book the way we so often read the Bible, choosing a sentence here and there, missing out large chunks altogether and skipping to our favourite bits.

When I was taught to read the Bible in context it did not diminish God's voice on the page, rather it blew it open; it expanded and challenged and thrilled me. Reading the gospels as books made them come alive as exciting historical narratives in which the authors had chosen their material and placed the events in a carefully constructed order inspired by the Holy Spirit to teach essential truths. Each book has its own structure and themes, what Dick Lucas referred to as its 'melodic line'. If we are to read the Bible seriously we should try to work out where the passage we are studying fits into this 'melodic line'. That is a daunting task indeed but not an impossible one. Some books lend themselves to being read in one sitting, others may take longer, but I encourage you to try to read whole Bible books – it is very rewarding!

Each passage is set not only within the context of its book but is placed in the gradual unfolding of God's story; each passage has not only an immediate context but also a larger biblical context. Therefore it is also essential to place passages in the context of the unfolding plan of salvation. For example, 2 Samuel 7 is all about the promise of a Davidic king to come, but we will not have studied the passage adequately unless we see that Jesus is this promised king. The more we read the Bible the easier this process becomes. However, we must take care that we do not cross-reference outside of the passage we are studying unless it is essential to help unlock the passage. In our groups a good rule of thumb is to only use other parts of the Bible to help us understand the passage we are reading when it is obvious from the text that we must do so, for example whenever the Bible quotes another book, character or event.

The Bible interprets itself!

It came as a great relief to me to discover that reading the Bible was not about trying to find a deep and obscure metaphorical meaning, but instead it was seeking to find the author's meaning using all the investigating tools that we have at our disposal. The Bible tells us what it means and we do not have to guess at it. For example, we are told: 'Christ died for our sins' (1 Corinthians 15:3) – Christ's death is an historical event and it is interpreted for us as being for our sins. Sometimes we need to read on further in a book to find an explicit reason that the author gives for writing his book. For example, John tells us that he wrote his gospel so that we 'may believe that Jesus is the Messiah, the Son of God, and that by believing [we] may have life in his name' (John 20:31). This comes at the end of the book but it provides a helpful framework for us as we consider why John recorded the events he did and it will help us as we seek to apply what he wrote. Not every book has such a clear authorial statement of intent but there are often clues that point to the purpose of the author. This is where noticing the literary form of a passage comes into its own: Old Testament narratives may use repetition of ideas and echo themes to highlight the important points, and psalms are poems which flag up key ideas through their very structure.

The key questions

Studying the Bible is both incredibly straightforward and simultaneously complex. For those of us who come to it with very poor reading habits or no reading habits at all it might feel daunting. But despite all the apparent complexity, whenever we read the Bible we are really doing just three simple things. These three things can be summarised in the following questions:

1. What does the passage say?

2. What does the passage mean?

3. What is the implication of this passage? (This is what I call the 'so what?' question.)

'What does it say' questions will involve close reading of the text, noticing all the words and details, patterns, repetitions, similarities and contrasts. 'What does it mean' questions will involve drawing out the larger context in the book and in Bible history but frequently returning to the text in front of you to check out what the passage says and why. The 'so what' questions take the truths of the passage to challenge us to listen and respond to God's Word.

In this chapter we have looked at some key elements that are involved in preparing a passage but these three questions form the heart of all our Bible study. They not only form the basis for our personal study but play an essential role in the study we prepare for our groups. The task for the leader is to gather everything that they have learnt from studying the passage and prepare questions for their group. This is our next challenge.

Useful books

The following titles will help you to learn more skills in studying the Bible:

→ Nigel Beynon and Andrew Sach, *Dig Deeper!: Tools to Unearth the Bible's Treasure* (InterVarsity Press, 2010).

→ Kathleen Bushwell Nielson, *Bible Study: Following the Ways of the Word* (P&R Publishing, 2011).

→ Gordon D. Fee and Douglas Stuart, *How to Read the Bible*

for All Its Worth (Zondervan, revised edition 2014).

➔ Gordon D. Fee and Mark L. Strauss, *How to Choose a Translation for All Its Worth* (Zondervan, 2007).

For a more detailed exploration the following is highly recommended:

➔ Andreas J. Köstenberger and Richard D. Patterson, *Invitation to Biblical Interpretation* (Kregel Academic, 2011).

Models of Bible studies

When it comes to sitting down and writing questions for a Bible study, most of us stare at a blank piece of paper and then decide to go to the nearest Christian bookshop to find something off the shelf that will give us an outline. In fact we don't need to go out of our house at all because many websites have questions for groups available online for free. These are valuable resources, but only if used with discernment and care. Every Bible study group comes with its own unique dynamic, and transferring something that works in one setting to another might not work. If we take published material straight into our own context without thinking it through for ourselves and our group members, we will short-change people; it is like a preacher not writing his own sermons and reading out the published sermons of others instead. A preacher can learn from reading sermons, and he may use others' ideas and illustrations, but he will need to prayerfully think through how to teach his own congregation.

It is very hard in a Bible study to use someone else's questions. I have sat in groups where everyone has spent ages trying to work out what the question in the book means. Study books with answers can be used as an arbitrating authority but in extreme cases create a situation where people stop looking at the Bible and just read the book. However, published material can give us confidence that we are on the right track, as well as providing helpful background material or really useful ideas on how to understand a passage. Some churches share the same studies across several home groups so that everyone in the church is looking at the same part of the Bible at the same time. When using generic material, though, we need to keep in mind what we want to achieve in our studies in order to understand the strengths and weaknesses of the approaches that these published studies use. I am going to look at some of the common forms that these studies take.

The detailed study

This contains many detailed questions that go through the passage, often taking each verse in turn. The vast majority of the questions tend to be the discovery type, for example: 'Where is Jesus in verse 1? What does He say in verse 2?' This model is very common but it is quite dull. It frequently creates long pauses as everyone waits for each other to say the obvious. However, discovery questions are useful and these can help people *really* read the passage. It is amazing what details we miss when we read the Bible, and discovery questions are particularly useful for groups that struggle to engage with the details of a passage on first reading.

Nevertheless, discovery questions are weak on helping people think through what is or is not important, and there is a danger that big ideas get lost in a multitude of answers. Frequently this model of study allows little room for discussion, with people answering politely almost as though they were answering comprehension questions in a school test. It is hard to engage with group members because everyone becomes concerned to have the 'right answer' and they can become afraid to speak in case they get it 'wrong'.

Despite the failings of this model we often graduate towards doing our studies this way because it feels safe; it gives the leader control because there is no room for someone to go off on a tangent, and we feel we have done the passage justice because we have covered it all. However, this approach provides limited room for someone to dig deeper.

Overall this model helps us get to grips with what a passage says but frequently fails to get to the main ideas and help a group think through the implications. Lists of questions highlight the different 'trees' in the wood, but we need to stop and look at the wood as a whole in order to get a true perspective. So although detailed questions will form a part of our study, we will need to take a step back and find a way of drawing everything together. Part of our job as a leader is to decide which questions will help us get to the heart of a passage. In our preparation we will have asked ourselves all sorts of questions which failed to help us get to grips with the passage, but we will have discovered other questions which were important in deepening our understanding – it is these questions that should form the backbone of our study.

The chunk study

The chunk study is a study that avoids the pitfalls of the detailed study by dividing the text into sections, drawing a main point from each and applying each part as it goes along. This structure comes from a great heart. It comes from the leader who is concerned for God's Word to be experienced as relevant and practical. Some published Bible study materials go for this approach to stop people losing interest while studying a large portion of text, but it can be at the cost of the overall point of the passage. It is artificial to push an application point at the end of each section unless the passage is teaching it. The application of a text comes from understanding what a passage is communicating; it is the passage that should dictate the point at which it is important to stop and ask the 'so what' question.

For example, when studying Luke chapter 1 it is helpful to stop and think through the significance of Luke's introduction in the first four verses before going on to read about John the Baptist's birth. This is because the writer has written it as a prologue. Then, as the chapter develops, there is value in reading a large chunk at a time before putting the whole thing together. The reason for this is that the meaning becomes clearer when all the narrative is read, and even sharper when both birth announcements are compared. Each story can be looked at individually, but there is great gain in looking at the flow of events and the different responses to the message of the angel. If we stop too soon we break the flow of the narrative, which can stop us from seeing the larger picture. Our model of Bible study should match the flow of the passage; let the 'big idea' of the passage dictate the structure of our studies.

The application study

This is a very popular model in published materials. The study begins with a scenario to discuss, posing a challenging question designed to get a group talking about the main issue of the passage right from the start. Such questions often function as warm-up questions for the group. Yet the difficulty with some warm-up questions is that they try to get the group to discuss personal issues very early on, before these are then addressed in the study. Sometimes they set people up to fail by making them expose their wrong thinking publicly. I have used warm-up questions myself in Bible studies but have since come to the conclusion that they are generally unhelpful and a bit unkind. Another problem with this model is that it dictates the application and therefore has already committed the group to a line of thought before the Bible has even been looked at. Alternatively a danger of the application study is that the leader uses it to push their own agenda and stops people freely meditating on God's Word and discovering the 'big idea' for themselves.

Recently I was with a youth leader who wanted to address the subject of alcohol addiction with his youth group, so he planned to use the passage about Noah's drunkenness (Genesis 9:20–23) to say that Noah was an alcoholic. Aside from the error of reading into the text more than it tells us, using a passage in this way stops the group from understanding what the passage is really there for. I have done similar in my time, for example when studying Mark 1:16–20 which is an account of Jesus calling His disciples. I have begun by asking the group what they find difficult about sharing the gospel with others; this presupposed an interpretation of the passage and gave a heavy indication that I thought this passage should encourage us to evangelise others. Treating Scripture in this way is like caging a wild lion that should be free. We need to be very careful to allow God to speak through His Word and not restrict it to our own limited horizons.

The strength of this application approach, though, is that it builds in a warm-up time before going straight into reading the Bible. This is helpful. It is important for a group to be comfortable with one another before a study begins; the more relaxed the group, the more people will engage with the text and each other. But the best way to achieve this is to form strong relationships with each other so that in an atmosphere of trust you can grapple with a passage together. The most effective Bible studies I have been in are those with close friends, and without doubt reading the Bible with my husband has been best of all. In our churches we have all kinds of Bible study groups and it may not be possible for the group to know each other well, but finding a way to help people feel comfortable and safe together as quickly as possible is important. One of the greatest ways is to provide a social time before studying the Bible; eating with one another is ideal, yet even having tea and coffee gives people a chance to chat. The better the relationships in the group, the more possibility there is that people will feel comfortable joining in a small-group discussion.

The open study

This type of study is not available as published material but if you were to Google 'Bible study approaches' many of the models that you find come into this category. One such is the Vasteras model developed in Sweden by a pastor in a rural congregation. In this model there are five steps to help encourage personal reflection, group discussion and sharing as outlined below:

Step 1:   Read the passage aloud as a group.

Step 2:   Each individual reads the passage again and makes the following marks in the margins:

    i: This is new for me – a new understanding, new insight, new appreciation.

    ii: I want to remember/memorise this verse/idea.

    >:   This strikes me as being especially important.

    ?:   This is not clear. I need help in understanding what it says.

Step 3:   Each person selects two or three markings to share with the group.

Step 4:   Together, share markings and discuss questions, new insights and application to life.

Step 5:   Each person concludes the study with a statement of personal response.

There are huge strengths in this, particularly in one-to-one studies.[14] It actively encourages everyone to connect with the Bible passage; it enables each person to identify where they are at in their understanding; and it is committed to everyone having a personal response to God's Word. Its weakness comes from the fact that no one takes responsibility to help the group move further on in their understanding, which reinforces the notion that there are a variety of valid and even contradictory interpretations of a text. But if a leader who has studied the passage beforehand is prepared to ask questions to clarify ideas and develop understanding, this could work well at helping one another dig deeper into God's Word.

In the next chapter I will outline an approach to help leaders begin to write their own material so as to enable people to really engage with the text and move further on in their understanding and relationship with God. The aim is to develop an approach that builds on the strengths of all of these methods in order to help people *really* read the Bible together and to hear God's voice.

The 'big question' model

The good news is that working out questions for a Bible study is not difficult because basically every Bible study is made up of the same three questions! Actually there are a couple of extra tweaks that I add but it came as a great relief to me that putting a study together was not an exercise in imaginative creativity. Our group Bible studies should basically model the way we approach reading and studying the Bible when we are on our own. This means the key questions are still: 'what does it say?'; 'what does it mean?'; and 'what are the implications of these truths?' or the 'so what?' question. These are the key questions that we looked at in chapter 3:

1. What does the passage say?

2. What does the passage mean?

3. What is the implication of this passage?

The first two questions help the group to *really* read the passage and understand it, which leads them to the 'big idea'. Once the 'big idea' is clear, the 'so what?' question follows naturally. Questions do not have to be clever but they do have to help people look at what the Bible says with the expectation that it will have an impact on their life. These three questions are always very useful in helping groups read a text faithfully, and provide a discipline and framework for developing good Bible-handling skills.[15]

As we become more confident preparing our studies, we will begin to notice the few key questions that helped us identify the main points of the passage while we were studying on our own. Using these questions forms the basis of the 'big question' model. It aims to engage with the text by using a few carefully chosen questions to enable discussion. Discussion is the key to revealing the current understanding of the group, thus helping one another develop a more biblical one.

The 'big questions'

The 'big questions' are linked to the 'big idea' in the passage. To demonstrate this, here are the questions I used for a study in Genesis 3:

↳ Q. 1. What was the process that led to Adam and Eve eating the forbidden fruit?

This question is a 'what does it say?' or discovery question. To answer it people needed to look back carefully over the first six verses. This exercise can be done as a large group or by breaking people up into smaller groups which later feed back their discoveries to the group as a whole. I generally prefer to break into small groups as it helps involve everyone. As people answered there was discussion about what the details implied and their significance, which led naturally to the 'what does it mean?' and 'so what?' questions.

↳ Q. 2. What were the consequences of their sin?

This is also a discovery question but it helped focus the discussion about what the details the group had discovered meant. The group looked backed to the first six verses and then on to more details in the passage. The consequences of human rebellion in Genesis 3:7–24 is a long list but each time we looked at one we did not need to do anything more sophisticated than ask 'what does this mean?'. For example, we had a long discussion about what it meant that Adam and Eve realised they were naked (verse 7). This passage raised lots of issues and many of my group had a variety of ideas and perspectives on it from various places including literature and art. Therefore in our discussion we had to keep looking back at the passage to see if our understanding fitted with what the Bible said.

↳ Q. 3. How does this chapter help us understand God and the world in which we live?

This was my 'so what?' question designed to help people focus on the things that struck them and to begin to think them through. It was deliberately directed away from individual application at this point. (We will look at detail at application in chapter 6.)

My three 'big questions' were drawn from the 'big ideas' in Genesis 3 concerning the rebellion of humanity and God's consequential judgement. The 'what does it say?' questions aimed to look in detail at the process of human rebellion and its consequences. The 'what does it mean?' questions followed on closely behind as each detail was discovered. In this study I used the 'what does it say?' questions to unpack the details of the passage and then simply asked the group 'what does that mean?' as it is a passage that lends itself to lots of discussion even as the details are being drawn out.

In summary, good 'big questions':

→ Are understandable.

→ Are easy to absorb.

→ Get a group looking at the text.

→ Draw attention to significant details.

→ Help a group discover the main point.

→ Open up discussion and have several valid answers.

→ Enable lots of people to contribute.

Questions to avoid are:

→ Questions that can be answered without looking at the text.

→ Questions that demand one-word answers.

→ Long and complicated questions.

→ Questions that contain jargon or technical terms.

The 'big question' model in action

The moment of truth arrives as the group settles down to begin a study; for some of us this is the hardest moment. Thoughts that flash across my mind are: 'Will I be able to engage everyone? What if they ask about that bit in the passage I'm still not sure of? Will what I have prepared work? Will it be useful?' I am sure that everyone feels nervous and inadequate at times when it comes to leading the study. I preach to myself that God is Sovereign, His Word is powerful, and He works despite me! It is a joy to know that God is the One we are seeking to listen to and He does speak through His

Word – it is this truth that gives me the confidence to dare to teach.

Despite all our preparation we cannot help others accept the truth of God's Word – that is a work of the Spirit, but a work that God longs to do. So prayer is a vital place to start when we read the Bible together. I rejoice that God's Word is not chained and I pray that all of us will hear and listen to God's voice as we read the Bible together.

It seems strange now but there was a time when I expected everyone to read the passage before coming to the study and somehow manage to plunge straight into answering questions without reading it aloud at all. I thought it saved time and gave us longer for our study. It was listening to poetry readings that changed my mind. I realised the value of listening to the written word read aloud; it brings nuances to the ear that often we miss when we are reading silently. I now consider reading the Bible aloud to be an essential part of listening to God's voice.

In practice this means the Bible should be read by one person so as not to interrupt the flow of a passage, or at the most broken up by two voices but only when the passage switches to a new idea. Reading the passage round the group by people who do not like reading aloud can destroy its meaning. I confess I have done this and by the time we have finished reading round no one has heard a word that has been said! Nevertheless, even though you know that it may not be read as well as you would like, sometimes it is helpful to have people read the passage aloud to help them gain confidence in engaging with the Bible. In groups like these it is worth reading the passage twice using a second reader, thereby enabling people to stop and listen again. If you do this, though, establish it as a normal pattern rather than making the first reader feel that they have failed. Indeed it is often helpful to read the passage more than once; it establishes a really important principle – God's Word is worth listening to with great care. Hearing the passage is vital.

After reading the passage I have a standard opening question other than the 'big questions' I have already outlined and I introduce it either the first time the passage is read out or on a second reading. The question is: 'what strikes you as you listen to this?' This is the 'no-holds-barred' question.

↳ The 'no-holds-barred' question

No-holds-barred is apparently a nineteenth-century wrestling term, which may be quite an apt description for a question that allows everyone in the group to grapple with the text and say whatever they like. I used to be anxious that if I allowed an open question, the discussion would quickly get out of control and leave the text behind. In practice I have discovered that when a group explores the passage with complete freedom, we come to an understanding of the whole faster.

The 'what strikes you?' question is a variation of the Vasteras model which we looked at in chapter 4. It can be useful to give everyone in the group a paper copy of the passage on which they can mark particular thoughts but then to ask everyone to share what things stood out for them – although for others this can feel too academic. Variations of this question include: 'what things do you think are particularly important?' or 'what things seem difficult?' It enables the group to highlight complicated, unfamiliar and challenging ideas as well as the familiar. Allowing a 'no-holds-barred' approach raises early on things that individuals really struggle with.

Recently I was studying 1 Thessalonians chapter 2 with a group and one person mentioned at the 'no-holds-barred' point that they thought Paul came across as bigheaded – he seemed to be so sure of himself. As the study progressed, this question helped us all to grapple with why Paul was writing his letter and enabled us to discover that his motivation was to encourage the Thessalonians that the gospel message they had heard was the truth and that it was worth them keeping on going despite suffering – something we realised was important for us too! Frequently I am amazed at the times using this simple question draws out the most essential things in the passage, although I shouldn't be.

Using the 'no-holds-barred' approach allows the leader to identify early on where an individual's understanding is before going back into the detail of the passage. If you remember the illustrations about hermeneutics in chapter 2, this exercise at the beginning of the study identifies the 'gorillas' that people have spotted; it shows the leader where people are on the hermeneutical spiral. It reveals if people are a long way back in their understanding of the passage or quite close to the heart of it. I write down everything that is raised on a large sheet to make sure these issues are covered during the study. Normally the study does address these things, but if it hasn't, I will return to them at the end. It means that every group member has had an opportunity to have his or her own questions addressed. If concerns remain which the passage has not addressed, these can be discussed after the study, perhaps on a separate occasion on a one-to-one basis or as a group event looking at things over a meal that we haven't had a chance to discuss together during our studies.

⤷ The body of the study

As well as asking questions we need to listen to the answers that are given. This is one of the hardest things to do. After all your preparation and with a head full of ideas, it is easy to presume that everyone is on your own wavelength. Sometimes we are so keen to get through the study that we pounce on any answer given, anticipate what others will say and twist it a little to make it fit with our framework. It must be horribly frustrating for group members when we do this! *Really* listening to answers is a skill we need to develop, and the more confident we are in our relationships with the group, the easier it is. A group that is happy to grapple with a text together, and is not afraid of getting an answer wrong but is hungry to have their understanding deepened, is a joy to work with. Most groups are a mixture of the vulnerable and confident, shy and loud, clear and muddled, and most of us are a combination of all of this at different times. Being heard and listened to helps us belong, participate and learn.

A Bible study is not an exercise in English comprehension but an opportunity for individuals to come face to face with God's Word and for it to impact their lives. It is important to help group members explain their answers so that their understanding is sharpened; their answers can be developed to help them move on in their understanding. So encourage someone to say a little bit more; don't be content with half answers; get people to show everyone where their idea came from in the passage. For example, use comments such as: 'That's really helpful – can you push that idea further?' or 'Yes that's great, but what do you think "justification" (replace this with whatever technical word they just used) means?'

It helps to give group members feedback. However, it does not have to be done instantly. For example, after some discussion you can draw attention to a previous answer: 'So we can see that x was spot on when they said y.' We all need affirmation as well as correction. There are also times when we have to let comments stand unchallenged but continue to pray that God's Word will do its work. Recently in a study of mine a new group member offered her first tentative contribution: 'I think all religions lead to God.' How should this be addressed? It is not appropriate to jump on this comment and rip it to shreds there and then in a group. Doing that is not only unloving but risks the individual never speaking again and never coming again either. It flagged up to me, though, that I should meet up for coffee with her sometime and gently explore her understanding of the gospel. Yet on the night as a group we let the comment stand; the passage itself was doing the work of challenging her understanding. My desire is always to let the Bible be heard and trust that God will work in an individual's life.

↳ Can you lead a Bible study with just three questions?

In practice having prepared a study that uses the 'big question' model, you will use lots of other questions as well. These cannot be prepared beforehand because they are 'think-on-your-feet' questions, otherwise known as supplementary questions. This can sound terrifying – many of us find it hard to think on our feet – but basically they will always be based on the main questions:

→ What does it say?

→ What does it mean?

→ So what?

Knowing the right supplementary questions to ask will begin to come naturally as you start to listen to the group and help them get to grips with the passage.

Let us suppose that I began a study with the question: 'What was the process that led to Adam and Eve eating the forbidden fruit?' I may be met with complete silence. This silence has to be interpreted. There are several possibilities as to its cause:

→ They are waiting for someone else to speak.

→ They do not understand the question.

→ They are reading the passage and thinking about an answer.

This is when supplementary questions are needed. I have to make a guess about which cause applies. My first guess would be that my question is worded badly – so I reword it: 'What different things happened before Adam ate the fruit?' If the silence continues I point people to the text: 'Have a look at verses 1–6. What happened?' This last question is very basic and it is why I prefer not to start with a question like this, but no one minds simple questions that help clarify their thinking. If I still get no response because I have a group that does not like to talk aloud in a large group, I will break them up into smaller groups to tackle the same question. It is amazing how the conversation starts to flow. I try to avoid putting people in pairs, though, because this can put pressure on the silent individual who really wants to listen in.

Alternatively what would happen if I asked my discovery question and everyone began an animated discussion? I still need other questions for the following reasons and in the following ways:

→ To make sure the person who has answered understands their answer.

    ➜ 'Where do you get that from the text?'

➤ 'What do you mean by that?'

'Why do you say that?'

→ To make sure that everyone else in the group understands it.

➤ 'Can anyone else see that idea and explain it to us?'

→ To help them to engage with the text.

➤ 'How do you get that from the text?'

➤ 'How does that fit in with verse 3?'

➤ 'Show us how you got that idea?'

→ To summarise.

➤ 'Can anyone help us see where we have got to?'

➤ 'What are the main points we have got to so far?'

➤ 'Can someone sum up for us?'

→ To get the rest of the group into play.

➤ 'What does everybody else think about that?'

➤ 'Who else agrees with x? Why?'

This process will continue through the study. I have attempted to put it together as a flowchart – see Figure 1.

A Flow Chart of a Bible Study

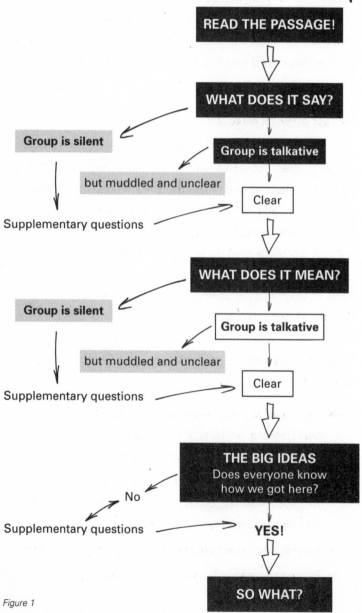

Figure 1

Each stage has either silence or talking, and both responses require 'think-on-your-feet' questions until the group has reached a point where they can move on to the next stage. A group cannot ask what a passage means until they have worked out what it says, and likewise they cannot begin to think about its application until they have understood what it means.

Can I use other techniques?

The 'big question' model, although it is centred on three basic questions, does not exclude using a variety of techniques within the study to help answer those questions. People have different learning styles and some find visual aids really helpful. The key question to ask yourself, though, is whether such techniques will help your group look at what the passage is saying. We must not let our respect for learning styles stop us from focusing on the words of the Bible. God has given us His truth in literary form and we need to work hard to help others access it, especially those who find reading a challenge.

With that warning, the following are just a few of the ideas that can be used:

→ Visual aids, e.g. large paper and coloured pens for brainstorming, or charts to fill in to show comparisons, similarities, differences, responses, etc.

→ Pre-prepared sheets of the themes and issues in the passage for the group to rank in order of importance and then discuss and defend their position.

→ Pre-prepared cards to put points of an argument into order.

→ Related preparation questions for the group to look at

in advance. This can be very helpful for some groups in enabling excellent discussions when you meet together.

As we have already discussed, splitting into buzz groups which then feed back to the large group is another method that can help include quieter members.

⤷ The 'so what?' question

The 'so what?' question is an opportunity for individuals to think through the implications of the truths they have discovered, which may change their view of God, the world and their lives. This question is of vital importance. We do not want our Bible studies to be an accumulation of knowledge; rather we want to grow up in maturity, to become more like Christ and to live our lives in service of our heavenly Father. However, if we rush this question we produce legalistic or clichéd answers.

We need to spend time meditating on the implications of the truths that we discover without reducing the truth to a simple rule to follow. God's Word is so much more profound than that. In our groups we may be able to share some of our first responses to a passage, but we need to allow the Word to really take root in our lives and to continue to meditate on it long after the study has finished. This is the subject of the next chapter.

⤷ Finally

One important way to allow the passage to take root in our lives is to begin to base our prayers on what we have just learnt. At the end of a study pray together as a group, particularly about what you have studied. As we pray in line with Scripture, it helps us align ourselves to God and His purposes. Our prayers are our first and immediate application of the passage. God has spoken to us through His Word, we listen carefully and we turn to Him in relationship through our prayers by responding to what He has said.

Meditating on God's Word

Many of us feel that getting to the application is the most important thing we do in our studies. We don't study God's Word to accumulate academic knowledge; rather we want to listen to God's voice and live in response to it. Our desire is for the group we are leading to be increasingly transformed into the image of Christ. However, this good desire sometimes leads us to force applications on to the text which are perhaps not there or are at best a minor point in the passage. We begin with good intentions, but in our enthusiasm we end up not really hearing God speak and instead push people into the issues we decide are important; it is as though we fear that God's Word is a bit ineffective without our help. But we don't need to manipulate the Bible to make it powerful. God's Word is living and active; it will feed us, equip us and challenge us (Hebrews 4:12; 2 Timothy 3:16–17). Our job in a Bible study is to do everything we can to help others hear and listen to God's Word so that they may know Him, but we cannot control how others will respond. Each believer has their own individual relationship with the Father; He will speak to them and His Spirit will work in their lives.

Our generation, like every generation before, suppresses the truth and knows nothing about God, yet the idea that the Bible is an instruction manual that tells us what to do is still common currency. Our culture believes that the Bible is a rule book: a list of restrictive dos and don'ts. But this is yet another way of suppressing the truth; it is vital we do not succumb to the same mentality and reduce the Bible to a list of clichéd instructions. The more I talk with students and listen to media, the more I hear people who have no knowledge of God at all. It is tragic. We have so much access to God's living, breathed-out Word and yet people do not know Him.

Reading the Bible together in small groups is a privilege and joy, and we do it primarily to listen to God and to get to know Him. Have you ever thought about the wonder of this?! So many seek a spiritual experience of some kind; we have the privilege of access to our Father, because of Christ, and we can continue to hear His voice through the Scriptures! Let's not make our studies into sessions that leave everyone burdened by religious rules but instead let us encourage each other to live in relationship with our Lord because of His mercy.

In practice the Bible is easily reduced to a few simple applications that are always true: fear God and worship Him alone; repent and believe; be holy and evangelise. These are drawn out in various ways and include teaching on meditating on the Word, prayer, worship, loving God, loving others, living as church, family responsibilities and participating in society. But despite all of this the Bible is mostly about God. The more we read it, the more we plunge into the depths of who God is and how He acts. Moreover, the problem we face when we read such truths about God is our tendency to want the Bible to be practical before we can believe it is relevant to us.

Most of us can easily turn to passages that are there to primarily teach us about God into legalism. Let's look at an example: Mark chapter 2:1–12 and the story of Jesus healing the paralysed man. The 'big idea' is that Jesus has the authority to forgive sins; it teaches us both about who Jesus is and what He has come to do, with some additional ideas such as the importance of dealing with sin and the religious rejection of Jesus. In view of this, see what you make of this 'so what?' question: 'Jesus makes forgiving sin a priority. Everyone needs to be forgiven. So what evangelistic opportunities have we got this week to help others hear this message?' This is definitely close to one that I have used myself. Of course it is good to encourage one another to evangelise and this question is quite close to the passage. But is it the most pertinent question? I have come to see that questions like this close the passage down. Instead of allowing God to speak truth to an individual heart, the 'big idea' is diminished into a 'work' by the leader through an overly directed question. This type of approach takes control of the text as if it were 'helpless without our help'.[16] It stops people engaging with the revealed truth on a personal level because the group leader has already decided that the group needs to be encouraged to evangelise. However, God's Spirit is the One who convicts us and speaks to our hearts, and who are we to second-guess the thing that will most speak into the heart of another? There may be people who need to be urged on to evangelise, but there may also be those who need to turn to Jesus for forgiveness; there may be those who need to repent of self-righteousness; there may be those who need to believe that Jesus can forgive even their sin; there may be those who need to come face to face with the idea that Jesus is God. I could go on and list many and various ways this truth could be applied to an individual.

Recently I spoke with a friend who was being told every week in their home group that he should evangelise. He was struggling with many family issues, serious ill health and bereavements, and was the main carer of frail elderly parents. Studying the Bible in the group he was in was becoming a burden; he felt second-class because he was not able to be involved in outreach events; he felt guilty and a long way from God. The Bible study he was part of was diminishing God's Word through its legalistic approach to application. What he needed to know was that God is good; that Christ understands our weakness; that he can flee to God for rescue and comfort. He needed gospel encouragement and instead was on the receiving end of Bible 'bashing' in every sense of the word.

So how should we approach application in small group studies? First we need to explore what the passage says and then look at what it means. Once this point is reached it is helpful to summarise the truths that the passage teaches. It is these truths that we want rooted in people's lives. How does that happen? Will it happen by a series of questions that take the truth in a practical direction? It can be helpful to have some practical discussion because it models to one another what it means in practice to follow Jesus, but this discussion is in danger of limiting the impact of a study. So what can we do? The solution is to change how we think about application; we must get rid of the idea that application is 'done' in group Bible study and instead think about the way God administers truth to our hearts over time. The 'so what?'question needs to become a question that dominates our lives, not just an hour a week in our Bible studies! We should encourage people to listen to the Bible when we are together and then learn to meditate on it prayerfully. Everyone in the group should be encouraged to go away and keep on thinking and praying about the passage. Application questions are useful in a study only if they are very broad and are used to help one another *begin* to think through general principles; group members ought then to go away and think about the particular implications for their own lives. This means, for example, that the 'so what?' questions for Mark 2:1–12 could focus on why it is important to know that Jesus has the authority to forgive sin and how understanding and believing that truth will impact us today.

In order for each person to be encouraged to respond to God's Word in their own particular situation, it helps to give people questions to take home to meditate on through the week. Over time folk will catch the habit and won't need these questions. Here is a list of meditation 'take-home' questions that can be useful:

→ 'Do I really believe this?'

→ 'If I really believed this, what difference would it make to my life?'

→ 'Does how I think about Jesus/God day to day fit with the picture of Him I have just read?'

→ 'Knowing this about Jesus/God, how should I respond to Him?'

→ 'How does knowing this about Jesus/God affect the way I view myself?'

→ 'How does knowing this about Jesus/God affect the way I view others?'

→ 'How does knowing this about Jesus/God affect the way I view the world?'

→ 'If I really understood this about Jesus/God, how would that affect my life?'

→ 'Is there anything I want to change in my life in view of this?'

Group leaders often complain that application is the thing that is squeezed out in their studies. When pressured for time, some even resort to stopping and moving straight to application. The problem with this is that unless you have come to an understanding of what the text is saying, it is impossible to ask the 'so what?' question. Groups are different and will come to different points of understanding; people with no previous knowledge of a text may take a long time to get to one key idea; others may discover deeper nuances. But unless some form of statement about what a passage means has been clarified, the group cannot move on (see Figure 1 in chapter 5). So let me be radical and suggest that we do not worry so much about doing application in our studies but instead think of our studies as times when we *really* read the Bible together and then go away and begin to ask the 'so what?' question more fully.

This is an approach similar to the classical Bible study method *lectio divina*, which Eugene Peterson explains: '*lectio divina* comprises four elements: *lectio* (we read the text), meditation (we meditate the text), *oratio* (we pray the text), and *contemplalatio* (we live the text).'[17] In our Bible studies we spend some time reading the text and working out together what it means; on our own we meditate on it, consider it prayerfully and begin to live it. Of course all these elements are much more interwoven than the above method suggests. As we grapple with understanding a text, we are meditating on it; as we finish our studies we will be able to pray through the things we have heard; and being together is an act of living out God's Word. However, the point still stands – the best application will happen outside of the group.

Listening to God's voice in Bible study will not always be a comfortable experience. The Bible is a two-edged sword which challenges and changes us (Hebrews 4:12). Tim Keller writes of our engagement with God in this way: 'Only if your God can say things that outrage you and make you struggle will you know that you have got hold of a real God and not a figment of your imagination – an authoritative Bible is not the enemy of a personal relationship with God, it is the precondition for it.'[18] The Bible is not a comfortable, easy read – it will confront people – and because of this our group Bible studies may not generally be the best place for people to talk through these struggles. In my experience it is very rare for individuals to open up and discuss deep convictions in a group unless the relationships are very strong (and I don't think this is purely British reserve). I know that God's Word hasn't finished impacting our lives when we close our Bibles and go home – in fact it is just beginning.

A young woman who has been part of my Bible study for two years said that she now has an urgency to evangelise her friends and is doing it. This came from her deep conviction that judgement day is a reality and we all need the rescue Christ brings. This change did not come in one study, or one sudden moment of realisation, but over many months studying in a group Romans, Mark, and 1 and 2 Thessalonians. Another young woman from the same Bible study group described how she is no longer putting herself in vulnerable scenarios with non-Christian friends; instead she is seeking to avoid temptation and learning to actively pursue her relationship with God. So in the same Bible study group one young woman has been challenged to witness to her friends, and another to avoid drunkenness and sexual immorality. God's Spirit confronts individuals in ways and over issues that we can never guess at.

I could not guess the ways God would work in the lives of these young women. Yet my task was to correctly handle the Word of truth and help them see what it said; God does the rest!

God's Word does achieve its purpose: it 'will accomplish what I desire and achieve the purpose for which I sent it' (Isaiah 55:11). Yet when we fail to see the changes in people's lives that we long to see, we doubt it is powerful at all and our solution is to become legalistic and controlling. This is a serious danger in any ministry.

One of the hardest parts of being a Bible teacher of any kind is that just when you think you have taught something, it becomes evident that no one has understood it, or they have forgotten it, or they remember but it seems to make no difference to their lives. This is one of the most frequent frustrations I hear from people when talking about Bible studies. There is huge concern that all that our studies achieve is head knowledge, with no real impact on people's actual lives and hearts. It is heartbreaking at times, I know! However, when faced with this we must remember two central things. The first is that God's timing is not the same as ours. As people listen to God's Word, He is working, transforming lives and bringing them to maturity for eternity. We get discouraged because we want people to change quickly, which happens sometimes, but more often than not believers grow into maturity slowly; the process is gradual and unseen, taking weeks, months and years.

When I see a photograph of my children taken a few years ago, I am always amazed by the changes that have taken place in each of them. My children grow around me but day to day they always look the same! God works in this way in our lives; one day we will look back and realise all that He has been doing. I love Susan Schaeffer Macaulay's description that teaching our children is like taking them to the beach and watching them learn to play in water and sand. She then says this:

In the same way, we let the children come to our Lord by letting them know about Him. We are careful to 'go to the beach'. We read an appropriate portion of God's Word to them regularly. They can read His Words, see that we have a King, Saviour, Helper, Friend. Later on, the thinking aspects – the realization that this is truth – will follow. But don't try to schedule how the child will feel, how he should react, when he should understand each step, etc. Get out of the way. Let the child, God, and His Word be alone together. Let them work out their own relationship.[19]

This stands as a truth not only for our children but also for all those we disciple. We live in a time of quick fixes and instant gratification, and want to see change every week, but God's concern is to bring people to eternity. What matters is giving our group members the foundation that they need to stand firm until that day when they see their Lord face to face. And meanwhile we want them to know God in a foundational way so that when life spirals out of control, in the face of great suffering, bereavement, redundancy, disability and death, they will stand firm and rooted like the man in Psalm 1:

That person is like a tree planted by
streams of water,
which yields its fruit in season
and whose leaf does not wither –
whatever they do prospers.

Psalm 1:3

71

Dramatic instant changes are not proof of lasting fruit. We should not assume that we have had a 'good' Bible study based on one or two discussions about practical application. In terms of results, what matters is lasting fruit. It is no accident that Mark's gospel puts Jesus' teaching on the parable of the sower at the beginning of his teaching to the disciples, because it is foundational for everyone in ministry. The disciples needed to understand it and so do we. Jesus made it clear that some will reject God's Word, others appear to accept it, and still others will grow and bear much fruit. Those who do not seem to change should not discourage us – there will be rejection of the gospel message that will be expressed in a variety of ways, but we can also anticipate real transformation and fruit in good soil. Our part is to help others hear God's Word; our part is to take them, in Susan Schaeffer Macaulay's metaphor, to 'the beach'. Let's not forget the principle of the parable of the sower.

People today talk about methods and approaches to make 'sticky Christians'. This is not our task. We cannot do it. We are called to faithfully handle God's Word, to teach and proclaim it, but we are not in control of the results. That bit is God's work and He changes people by His Spirit through His Word – He makes Christians 'sticky'. We can trust that God's Word is powerful and it does do its work.

Some church circles think that we need to move on from group Bible studies and find other more powerful, fresh expressions of doing church. After all, they argue, reading a book together is surely outdated! But we never outgrow our need to hear God's Word, and group Bible studies are an excellent way to help us *really* read it and listen carefully. My prayer is that we let God do His work through His Word in our times together as we sit around open Bibles with ears to hear and hearts to respond. Let it shape us.

Nuts and bolts

I regularly run seminars about 'How to lead small groups'. Having explained the 'big question' model, some similar questions come up. This chapter will address some of the common questions I have been asked as well as address some of the practicalities involved in leading Bible study groups, namely:

→ Does this method really work?

→ How do I avoid people talking without looking at the text?

→ Surely I need to know the Bible really well to lead a Bible study?

→ Can you use published material and still follow this model?

→ What about people who are not literate?

→ Does this model work in one-to-one Bible studies?

→ Should women lead?

→ Are men's and women's Bible study groups different?

→ What about different versions of the Bible?

→ What place does prayer have in Bible study?

Does this method really work?

Switching from a model of Bible study that asks many questions to one with far fewer is nerve-wracking – it is as though your security blanket has been taken away. It might appear structureless, but this method has a very clear structure. People are often concerned that with so few questions the group will quickly come to a staggering halt. In my experience this does not happen. Sticking with the big questions helps everyone in the group understand what is happening and where the study is leading. It engages everyone at their point of understanding and encourages them to move further and spiral deeper into the text. Open questions encourage people to contribute and to discuss more. In your study you are not trying to be original, creative or imaginative but to model the questions we need to ask when we sit under God's Word. At its best it helps people demystify Bible study. And yes it does work!

I have spoken to leaders who have switched to this approach and they have been really excited by the way their Bible studies have changed. I know UCCF staff who have implemented this with students as well as leaders of established home groups, and the feedback has been very positive. It has particularly helped in settings where people have been tentative about Bible studies in the past and now find that the Bible has opened up to them in a fresh way. My biggest joy is that it has encouraged people to read the Bible more. It is in response to those people that I finally agreed to write this book.

How do I avoid people talking without looking at the text?

Leading a study that has open questions brings with it the

concern that the group will get sidetracked and stop looking at the Bible. Once there is an atmosphere that encourages contributions, groups can easily get carried away. Recently I was leading a study on 2 Thessalonians 2 about judgement and the second coming when someone suddenly said: 'Oh, this is just like *The Last Battle*!' There then followed an enthusiastic appreciation of C.S. Lewis and a few light-bulb moments as some realised for the first time that *The Lion, The Witch and The Wardrobe* was an allegory about Jesus' death and resurrection. Does it matter that we digressed for a while? Absolutely not! We are engaged with reading the Bible together in relationships. Did I have to say: 'OK, enough about C.S. Lewis now and let's get back to 2 Thessalonians?' Yes I did! In our studies we will have to make judgements about where the conversation is going and occasionally pull the group back to the text.

I think the confidence to do this comes over time, but generally this approach to Scripture is a guaranteed way to keep looking at the passage. Sometimes during the 'what does it mean?' stage, people can get lost in the things they already know as they seek to understand a passage, and then end up talking about another idea that is true but isn't being explained in the verses that are in front of them. If you notice this, simply say: 'That is true but is this what *this* passage is teaching us?' – it usually brings everyone back on track and gets folk looking at the text again.

Surely I need to know the Bible really well to lead a Bible study?

The better we know our Bibles, the better teachers we will be. There are no shortcuts. If we presume to teach, we should be students of God's Word ourselves. However, it is important to remember that all of us are learning; we are on that asymptotic graph on a line curving down towards the truth of God, but we haven't arrived, we have not got it 'cracked'. If we think we know it all, that is far more dangerous than knowing we have a lot to learn. Those who presume to know everything are at risk of leading others astray, telling them what they think they know and stilting discipleship, both their own and others.

Of course it helps to know the passage as well as you possibly can, and the better you know it the more able you are to identify where others' understanding is weaker and to know the best way to direct them. But even when you are aware you have not understood all the nuances of a passage and there are parts you struggle to understand, by asking the three big questions you will get somewhere. We will need at times to say to a group: 'I'm struggling to understand this.' We are all spiralling into the text and seeking to know God better: we will not know everything! Knowing our weakness keeps us humble and means we will ask for help when we need it. Sometimes while I'm studying a passage in a group, they help me see things much more clearly, which is a wonderful spin-off of being God's family together.

If you are leading for the first time and have the choice, start by looking at parts of the Bible that are more familiar to you. If you have never led a study before, read a gospel – Mark is the shortest and at the end of this book you will find some simple outlines to start you off. But as you grow in understanding, tackle the more unfamiliar parts using the same basic model but bearing in mind the different types of literature found in the canon of Scripture. I love Old Testament narratives and have added some studies in 1 Samuel in the appendix to help you begin to look at more unfamiliar texts too.

The best leaders are those with a gentle and teachable spirit who love God's Word and love God's people; they have a heart for the truth and a willingness to serve. Knowing that you still have much to learn should inspire you to read the Bible more and seek to communicate God's truth to others better. Your Bible-handling and leading skills will improve over time but what is crucial to begin with is your heart. Do you love God and knowing Him through His Word? Do you love others and long to bring them to God's Word? If the answer is yes, then give it a go.

Can you use published material and still follow this model?

Yes, but the material will need adapting. The 'big question' model is generally a lot simpler than most published Bible studies. Published material is also of varying quality, though there are some excellent ones available. It may be best to use the material in your private study and adapt it for your group.

The best material will help you frame the 'what does it say?' and 'what does it mean?' questions, but in my experience the 'so what?' questions tend to be too prescriptive. Take a highlighter pen and mark the 'what does it say?' questions, use another colour for 'what does it mean?' and another for 'so what?'. You may then need to cross some questions out altogether or think of one that works better. By knowing the framework from the 'big question' model, you will be able to adapt material and lead a study that is engaging and clear.

My hope is that as you grow in confidence you will write your own studies. It will involve a lot of careful preparation studying the passage beforehand. But you know your group best and so are best placed to formulate the wording of questions in a way that they will relate to.

What about people who are not literate?

In recent years there has been a tendency to suggest that Bible study is only for those who are of a literary academic bent, and that people who struggle with literacy need to access God's truth through different media other than the written word. I rejoice in all the various media we can now use to help teach one another – DVDs, the internet, visual and audio equipment – but I fear that these approaches short-change those who cannot read the Bible for themselves, as though they cannot understand the deep things of God. William Tyndale, the translator of the Bible into English, is attributed to wanting the ploughboy to be able to access Scripture. This did not mean that he wanted the Bible to be dumbed-down but for them to read it for themselves.[20]

So how do we lead studies with those who struggle to read? I worked on a voluntary basis with a charity called The Reader Organisation based in Liverpool.[21] They run reading groups with people in a variety of settings, drug rehabilitation units, prisons, community centres, residential care settings, work places and schools. The people in the groups often have complex social problems and mental health issues. Many dropped out of the education system early and none would describe themselves as readers. But in reading-aloud groups, led by a trained facilitator, they are introduced to a wide range of literature including the likes of Dickens, Tolstoy, Shakespeare and Milton. The group members regularly read material that they never considered they could manage or would be relevant to them, yet their enthusiastic response is overwhelming. The passages that are read are printed out on sheets and then read aloud by a competent reader, often more than once, especially if it is a poem. At the beginning of a session it might be read twice; then after some discussion it would perhaps be read again in the middle; and to consolidate it may be read at the end. People who cannot read can listen!

This approach can be built into our group Bible studies. Why not read the passage more than once? It helps us all to hear it read aloud. If the discussion seems to be drifting away from the passage, read it again; and read it at the end so we focus our minds clearly again on God's Word, with the added bonus that it comes alive even more having spent time discussing it together.

My grandfather was born in 1900 to a poor working-class family in the East End of London. He had to leave school as a boy and received little education. He was a man who worked with his hands and was not a man who could be described in any way as academic or as a reader. Yet his love of God drove him to the Bible and it became the book of his life, the only book he read. The early Sunday school movement taught literacy by teaching the Bible, and Susanna Wesley famously taught all her ten children how to read by beginning in Genesis and working through the whole Bible. I know a man who has struggled with dyslexia and hated reading at school, yet his passion for the gospel has driven him to become a diligent Bible student and a great Bible study leader. Many others have a similar testimony. We must not assume that poor literacy skills means that a Christian cannot begin to read their Bible, and indeed it may be the catalyst that helps them begin to read.

Does this model work in one-to-one Bible studies?

The simple answer is yes. It is really useful to ask someone that you are reading one-to-one with: 'What strikes you as you read this passage?' and then take the conversation on from that point. If you have one or two other 'big questions' about the passage, it helps the conversation flow naturally as you both look at the Bible together.

The danger in one-to-one is that the person leading becomes a kind of guru who asks so many questions that the whole experience is intimidating. However, the 'big question' model enables the leader to keep in mind the direction of travel during a joint discovery of a text, and does not make the experience so prescriptive that the participant is overwhelmed and has no scope to express their views. Knowing that when we read the Bible we need to check what it is saying, ask what it means and then consider its implications is foundational, and there is no better way to read the Bible one-to-one than this!

Should women lead?

This is a contentious subject and it is something we all need to come to a mind on. There are those who do not consider it an issue at all – of course women can lead Bible studies, they say; why is it even a question? There are others that believe it is a form of authoritative teaching and therefore a woman should not lead a Bible study with men in it as, according to 1 Timothy 2:12, a woman is not permitted 'to teach or to assume authority over a man'. Understanding the context of this verse is key. Some believe that this is referring to teaching the gathered church and overall leadership responsibility; others that it means women should not teach men in any context. I cannot do justice to the arguments fully here but there are excellent resources available to help you consider this question in detail.[22]

Whatever position you come to on this issue, I believe that leading studies is still an important ministry for women because women teaching women the Bible in group studies is a great way to obey this injunction in Titus 2:3–5:

> Likewise, teach the older women to be reverent in the way they live, not to be slanderers or addicted to much wine, but to teach what is good. Then they can urge the younger women to love their husbands and children, to be self-controlled and pure, to be busy at home, to be kind, and to be subject to their husbands, so that no one will malign the word of God.

There is no better way to do this than by bringing women to God's Word! Women's Bible studies should be rigorous and handle the Bible well, though. There has been a tendency for some church women's groups to chat about almost everything but the Bible. (I know this from personal experience!) Women's groups can also become sentimental, emotional or gossipy and we must fight against this. John Piper once commented:

> Wimpy theology makes wimpy women! Wimpy theology does not give a woman a God who is big enough, strong enough, wise enough, or good enough to handle the realities of life in a way that enables her to magnify Him and His Son – it is not big enough! Wimpy theology does not give a granite

81

foundation of God's sovereignty underneath.[23]

We need women to lead other women in the serious study of the Bible so that they can grow in their knowledge and love of God and stand firm like the psalmist exhorts in Psalm 1.

I frequently lead mixed-sex Bible studies with my husband. I seek to submit to his leadership in our marriage, and group Bible studies have been a great place for us to serve together. He has encouraged me to study Scripture and values my thoughts on what I am studying. We discuss the passages in depth together; in fact if I held back from challenging some of his ideas, I would not be submitting to him! He wants me to use my gifts and it does not undermine him in anyway. I personally do not believe that when it is my turn to lead a Bible study, I am exercising authoritative teaching as outlined in 1 Timothy 2:12. I also believe I can lead a study and remain under the authoritative leadership of the pastor of our church.

Indeed the 'big question' model is a way of helping one another read God's Word together and exalting one another in Scripture, which is an outworking of Colossians 3:16: 'Let the message of Christ dwell among you richly as you teach and admonish one another with all wisdom ...' Leading and being an active part of a Bible study group is one way we can let the Word of Christ dwell in us as we teach and admonish one another.

Are men's and women's Bible study groups different?

They are not! In terms of content and seriousness in approaching God's Word there really should not be any difference. However, without falling into unbiblical gender stereotypes, I have had women cry in Bible studies whereas I haven't experienced that response from men, although one man became so angry he walked out of a study once! There can be a tendency as well in some women (not all) to apply the Bible too quickly and to relate to texts on an emotional basis. In contrast there can be a tendency in some men (not all) to be too competitive and delight in debate. When we lead groups – be they men's groups, women's groups or mixed groups – we need to get to know the people in our groups with all their different temperaments, so that we can together listen to God's Word and submit to it. The measure of a successful study is not whether or not someone was reduced to tears, or that we had a rigorous debate. It is whether we have heard God's voice.

Some churches separate the genders routinely for Bible study. I confess to finding this a little sad. Small groups are the ideal place to be church family together, male and female united in Christ, encouraging and exhorting one another as we submit to God's Word. Both men and women benefit from listening to each other in this setting; our different perspectives and responses can help sharpen us all up. So I would urge church leaders that they should not always separate the sexes – we need each other; studying the Bible together gives a solid foundation for our relationships; and it is particularly helpful for husbands and wives to study together. But there is a biblical mandate for older women to teach younger women, and a small-group Bible study is a great place to do it.

What about different versions of the Bible?

It really helps if everyone in the group uses the same version of the Bible, but in my experience they rarely do! I play this one by ear. Sometimes in my personal study I become aware that there are significant differences between translations. Studying the Bible in small groups is a place where we can learn about the importance of these differences. If I want everyone to see the difference, I will print off the passage so that we all read from the same text during the Bible study but also point out the way the versions differ. It is helpful to explain why we prefer one version over another, and it may even be necessary to fill people in on the Greek and Hebrew words so that they can see the decisions that translators have made. However, most of the time the meaning can still be discerned clearly even when the group is reading a mixture of versions.

What place does prayer have in Bible study?

Prayer is at the heart of what we do. When we study the Bible we are not running a book group; it is not like reading any other literature. The Bible is God's Word, so we pray that God will speak to us through it and give us ears to listen, and we pray that we will remember what we have heard and may live in response to it. My son was asked recently in a youth group: 'What is more important – prayer or reading the Bible?' How would you answer that? Surely it is a false dichotomy: we need to hear God's voice and respond to Him; both are central to our relationship.

We should respond to a study with prayer. However, there can be a risk that when asking people what they would like to pray about, this turns into a long information-sharing session with often little relation to the passage; before you know it, everyone seems to have forgotten what was just studied. Instead of remembering God's Word we find ourselves talking about difficulties at work, illness, mortgage repayments, travel arrangements and so on. One solution to this is for the group to share the things they would like to pray for before the Bible is studied. This is especially helpful if someone is anxious about something when they arrive; it gets things off their chest and enables them to concentrate more on the passage during the study. It helps relationships too because when people have opened up with each other in this way, they generally find it easier to talk about the Bible together. You can then start the study after one person has briefly prayed for all the things everyone has mentioned. These things can be returned to and prayed about more at the end with the bonus of praying about them in light of the passage that has just been studied. We can bring all our concerns to God with a fresh focus, emboldened, challenged and refreshed by the truth of what we have read in His Word – God's Word really changes perspectives!

Whenever you choose to pray together as a group, it is vital to pray together and in particular allowing space for a submissive and thankful response to what you have read in God's Word.

Epilogue

Unleash the Word! Get together with others; open up the Bible; explore what it says and what it means; and respond to it in obedience. It is the way God speaks to us.

So many who profess faith fail to read the Bible, particularly on their own; reading it with others is so helpful. We have a famine of God's Word today, yet we live in an age when we have the opportunity to access it more than ever! Many Christians are seriously malnourished while the un-churched have lost cultural background knowledge of the Bible; one English professor I know, at Liverpool University, frequently bemoans the fact that none of his students can identify biblical allusions in literature anymore, but many churched folk have lost it too. I have read the Bible with young people who come from a Christian background but have never read or been read the resurrection accounts of Jesus, and certainly have no knowledge of the Old Testament. What riches they are missing!

We also need to study the Bible well in our small groups because we must not only unleash the Word but defend it. In the sixteenth-century the Reformation leaders fought to establish the authority of the Word over the authority of the church. In the twentieth century, evangelicals stood up for the credibility of the Word against modernist liberals who denied the miraculous and the possibility of its truth. In the latter part of the twentieth century there was a need to stand up for the sufficiency of the Word against those who believed the Spirit brought fresh revelations that were separate from the Word. But today there is a battle over how we understand it. The battles we face today have arisen from postmodernist thinking and are over how we interpret the Word. Many of the current debates over the role of women in the church, gay marriage and hell are not coming from those who say they deny Scripture but from those who say that they interpret it differently. But when God's Word, which is a two-edged sword, cuts, they change the Word to stop it hurting! Or, more dangerously, they just read a little bit of the Bible in isolation and lose the sense of the whole. We need to be equipped in this battle – we need to know how to listen to God's voice through Scripture and not make His sword blunt!

There is a right way to read the Bible! Small-group Bible studies are a way of helping one another to correctly handle the Word of truth against those who affirm it but interpret it with a twenty-first-century mindset. When we lead Bible studies we are helping others interpret what the passage is saying, modelling the questions we should ask of a text and submitting to its authority. The Bible is God's Word and can stand up to our most rigorous scrutiny. The more we read the Bible as a whole, not missing anything out, the more we see how it fits together. We must help each other do this.

Leading a Bible study is hard work but it is also a huge privilege. God speaks through His Word – what a joy! If we fail to take people to His Word, we are failing to take them to our Lord. Let us help one another more and more to meet with our Lord. Let us help others to engage with the joy we know of hearing our Lord's voice, of being given food for the soul that always sustains and nourishes. Let us be like Philip and say to others: 'Come and see' (John 1:46)! God's Word is powerful: let us unleash it!

Five 'big question' Bible studies in Mark

Here are five simple study outlines using the 'big question' model. I have used these when teaching group leaders the simplicity of the big question model. They are from the first few chapters in Mark's gospel as it is reasonably familiar material for many. In my training sessions people are frequently surprised by the amount of discussion so few questions elicit. The questions in italics are key questions. The other questions may or may not be helpful depending on how the discussion develops. The 'thinking it through' questions are to encourage people to continue to meditate on the passage after the group study.

STUDY 1: MARK 1:1-15

INTRODUCTION: THE 'NO-HOLDS-BARRED' QUESTION

→ *Is there anything that particularly strikes you as we read the passage through?*

WHAT DOES IT SAY?

→ *List all the different things Mark tells us about Jesus.*

→ *List all the different things Mark tells us about John.*

WHAT DOES IT MEAN?

→ *How does Mark interpret these things? Why does he include the details he chooses?*

→ In what ways does John prepare the way for Jesus?

→ Who is Jesus shown to be at His baptism?[24]

→ What do we learn from the brief mention of Jesus' temptation?

→ *Summarise everything that Mark has claimed for Jesus.*

SO WHAT?

→ Why do you think this is important?

→ Is there anything in this passage that points to how we should respond?

THINKING IT THROUGH (QUESTIONS TO CONSIDER ALONE)

→ *Who do I think Jesus is?*

→ *How does Mark's introduction fit with my understanding?*

STUDY 2: MARK 1:14-28

INTRODUCTION: THE 'NO-HOLDS-BARRED' QUESTION

→ *Is there anything that particularly strikes you as we read the passage through?*

WHAT DOES IT SAY?

→ (Print out a copy of the passage for every group member.) *Using the sheet mark any words or ideas that are repeated through the passage.*[25]

WHAT DOES IT MEAN?

→ *Why does Mark repeat these words?*

→ *Why does he place these stories in this way?*

→ *What are the most important aspects of Jesus' ministry in this passage?*

SO WHAT?

→ *What sort of responses does Jesus get in this passage?*

→ How do people respond to Jesus today? Why?

→ *Is there anything in this passage that points to how we should respond?*

THINKING IT THROUGH (QUESTIONS TO CONSIDER ALONE)

→ *How do I respond to Jesus?*

→ *What aspects of Jesus' ministry do I think are most significant?*

→ *How does my perspective of Jesus line up with the Jesus Mark wants me to know?*

STUDY 3: MARK 1:29-45

INTRODUCTION: THE 'NO-HOLDS-BARRED' QUESTION

→ *Is there anything that particularly strikes you as we read the passage through?*

WHAT DOES IT SAY?

→ *What ideas/words are continued from Mark's opening so far?*

→ *What new ideas/events are introduced here?*

WHAT DOES IT MEAN?

→ *Why does Jesus pray?* [26]

→ *Why does Mark include the private healing story?*

→ *Why does Jesus tell this man to go to the priest?* [27]

→ Why does Jesus tell the demons and man not to speak of what He'd done?

→ In what way do these different events link together?

SO WHAT?

→ *What does this passage show us about Jesus' priorities?*

THINKING IT THROUGH (QUESTIONS TO CONSIDER ALONE)

→ *Do I understand what Jesus' priorities were?*

→ *How should knowing Jesus' priorities affect my life and my relationships with others?*

STUDY 4: MARK 2:1-17

INTRODUCTION: THE 'NO-HOLDS-BARRED' QUESTION

→ *Is there anything that particularly strikes you as we read the passage through?*

WHAT DOES IT SAY?

→ What links are there in this section to the chapter before?

→ What new ideas are introduced here?

→ *List everything Jesus does in verses 1–17.*

WHAT DOES IT MEAN?

→ What do you make of the phrase 'when Jesus saw their faith' (verse 5)?

→ What do you make of Jesus' comment to the paralysed man?

→ What do the scribes object to in verses 13–15? Why?

→ *Why does Jesus heal the paralysed man?*

→ *What is Jesus teaching the Pharisees?*

→ How does the second story reinforce Jesus' priorities?

SO WHAT ?

→ *Why is forgiveness so important?*

THINKING IT THROUGH (QUESTIONS TO CONSIDER ALONE)

→ Do I understand what Jesus' priorities were?

→ How should knowing Jesus' priorities affect my life and my relationships with others?

→ Do I believe Jesus has authority to forgive my sin?

→ How should knowing Jesus has forgiven me affect my life and my relationships with others?

STUDY 5: MARK 2:18 – 3:6

INTRODUCTION: THE 'NO-HOLDS-BARRED' QUESTION

→ *Is there anything that particularly strikes you as we read the passage through?*

WHAT DOES IT SAY?

→ *In groups list the accusations Jesus faced.*

→ What is the underlying charge?

→ *How does Jesus answer each accusation?*

WHAT DOES IT MEAN?

→ *What do Jesus' answers reveal about Himself?* [28]

→ *Summarise everything Jesus has claimed for Himself and what He is doing.*

SO WHAT?

→ *Why do the religious leaders hate Jesus so much?*

→ What relevance does this have to us?

THINKING IT THROUGH (QUESTIONS TO CONSIDER ALONE)

→ Do I understand what Jesus came to do?

→ Why do I think Jesus received so much opposition?

→ What religious activities do I like?

→ Am I at risk of rejecting Jesus?

Eight 'big question' Bible studies in 1 Samuel

Introduction

These studies are a series of eight that cover the second half of 1 Samuel. They have been prepared using the following resources:

→ *1 Samuel: Looking for a Leader* by John Woodhouse (Wheaton, Illinois: Crossway, 2008).

→ *1 Samuel: Looking on the Heart* by Dale Ralph Davis (Tain, Scotland: Christian Focus Publications, 2003).

I have also used John Woodhouse's structure of the book, namely:

→ Chapters 1–7: The leader God provided.

→ Chapters 8–15: The leader the people asked for.

→ Chapters 16–31: The leader according to God's heart.

The following studies focus on 'the leader according to God's heart' (chapters 16–31).

Outline

General remarks

Although these studies focus on the second half of 1 Samuel, it is important that the context of the book as a whole is not forgotten. If necessary the first two studies could be done together in week one as a general introduction to the book, although this would be a lot of material to cover! Ideally it would be good to have another week at the end of the studies to review the big ideas from the book and to give people a chance to share some of the things that they have discovered through them.

1 Samuel is a historical narrative and therefore some of the studies cover a large amount of material. It is important to read the whole of each passage. The studies are designed to help people pick out the main ideas and themes that run through the narrative.

Themes in 1 Samuel

→ Leadership.

→ The establishing of the Messiah.

→ The qualities of God's leader.

→ The king who is promised, needed, rejected and rescued.

→ Strength and weakness.

→ The reversal of fortunes.

→ Opposition and suffering.

→ Trust in God.

Understanding 1 Samuel

It is very easy for Bible study groups to look at the life of David and see his life as an example of Christian discipleship. However we need to remember that Jesus said the Old Testament Scriptures were primarily about Himself (Luke 24:27). 1 Samuel is the book that introduces us to the Messiah – the Lord's 'king'; 'his anointed' (1 Samuel 2:10) – and is here to teach us primarily about the sort of king God promised. As we look at the life of David we will discover much about the life of Jesus!

The psalms link with the narrative in 1 Samuel and provide a further commentary. Read these psalms during your group time together or encourage your group to read them during the week.

STUDY 1: INTRODUCTION TO 1 SAMUEL

PART 1

→ *1 and 2 Samuel begin and end with two significant prayers, forming a helpful narrative arch: Hannah's prayer (1 Samuel 2:1–10) and David's (2 Samuel 22:1–51). Read these prayers.*

→ *What are the big ideas in each one?*

→ *What are the similarities between them?*

→ *What do you think is the key idea?* (In particular compare 1 Samuel 2:10 with 2 Samuel 22:51.)

PART 2

→ *God will have a faithful leader but ... read Judges 21:25; 1 Samuel 2:12; 3:1; 8:1–9. What was the situation in Israel at the beginning of the book?*

PART 3

→ *God gives them a king but ... read 1 Samuel 8:19–22; 10:24; 12:12–15; 13:8–14; 15:26–27, 35. What is the problem with the king the people have chosen?*

→ (Optional: There was provision in the law for a king – see Deuteronomy 17:14–20. What should he be like?)

SUMMARY

God gave the people the type of king that they asked for (1 Samuel 12:13) but in the second half of the book God begins to establish the king He wants: someone 'after his own heart' (1 Samuel 13:14).

STUDY 2: 1 SAMUEL 16:1-23

INTRODUCTION: 'THE NO-HOLDS-BARRED' QUESTION

→ What strikes you as we read the passage through? What stands out as surprising, encouraging or difficult?

16:1-13: WHAT DOES IT SAY?

→ List everything Samuel does.

→ List everything that the Lord tells Samuel.

16:1-13: WHAT DOES IT MEAN?

→ What does the Lord need Samuel to learn?

→ Compare 16:7 with 13:14.[29]

16:14-23: WHAT DOES IT SAY?

→ What notable events happen to David in this chapter?

16:14-23: WHAT DOES IT MEAN?

→ Compare David and Saul.

→ What is the significance of Saul's dependency on David?

→ What does this chapter teach us about God's anointed king?

→ What parallels are there here to Jesus' life and ministry?

SO WHAT?

→ Do you view the world from your perspective or God's?

→ How can you begin to see things from God's perspective?

→ What do you understand about God's purpose and plan for the world?

→ Do you believe that Jesus is God's anointed king?

→ What difference does it make to your life that Jesus is God's chosen king?

STUDY 3: 1 SAMUEL 17:1-58

This chapter is in the centre of the book, placed not in chronological order but theologically – it shows the anointed king-in-waiting acting to rescue God's people.

INTRODUCTION: 'THE NO-HOLDS-BARRED' QUESTION

→ *What strikes you as we read the passage through? What stands out as surprising, encouraging or difficult?*

WHAT DOES IT SAY?

→ *In small groups list everything we learn in this chapter about Goliath and David. Report back your findings.*

WHAT DOES IT MEAN?

→ *Why does David act as he does?*

→ *In what ways does this story illustrate the truths contained in Hannah's prayer (1 Samuel 2:1–10)?*

→ *What does this story show us about how God saves?*

→ *What does this teach us about how the anointed king saves?*

SO WHAT?

→ *How do you view the cross and the work of Christ? (See 1 Corinthians 1:18.)*

→ *Do you really believe that Jesus' saving work is powerful?*

→ *What things tempt you to doubt it?*

→ *In the face of those who defy God, how do you feel?*

→ *If you really believed that God will destroy His enemies, what difference would it make?*

STUDY 4: 1 SAMUEL 18:1 – 20:42

INTRODUCTION: 'THE NO-HOLDS-BARRED' QUESTION

→ *What strikes you as we read the passage through? What stands out as surprising, encouraging or difficult?*

WHAT DOES IT SAY?

→ *In chapters 18–19 what qualities does David have? What is emphasised?*

→ *Trace the different responses there are to David.*

→ *In what ways does God protect David?*

→ *In chapters 18–19 trace Jonathan's attitude to his father and to David.*

WHAT DOES IT MEAN?

→ *Why does Saul hate David so much? (See 20:31.)*

→ *What is the significance of the covenant between David and Jonathan?*

→ *Who needs whose protection?*

SO WHAT?

→ *What is your response to God's anointed king?*

→ *What makes you feel secure?*

→ *What matters to you most: your world here and now or Jesus' kingdom?*

→ *What does putting your allegiance to Jesus first in your life look like in practice?*

FOR FURTHER MEDITATION

Read Psalm 5.

STUDY 5: 1 SAMUEL 21:1 – 22:23

INTRODUCTION: 'THE NO-HOLDS-BARRED' QUESTION

→ What strikes you as we read this passage through? What stands out as surprising, encouraging or difficult?

WHAT DOES IT SAY?

→ To whom/where does David flee in chapters 21–22?

→ What is the outcome of each encounter?

→ Compare Saul and David. What concerns them and how do they relate to others?

WHAT DOES IT MEAN?

→ Was Ahimelech right to help David? How does Jesus understand this? Why does Jesus quote this story in Mark 2:23–28?

→ What does Saul teach us about being against God's anointed one, i.e. being anti-Christ?

→ How do these events fulfil 1 Samuel 2:27–33?

→ What does this teach us about God's sovereignty and human responsibility?

→ Where does safety lie? (See 22:2, 22–23.)

SO WHAT?

→ How is rejection of Christ seen in today's world?

→ Do you trust that God is in control even when bad things happen to good people?

→ Do you understand that suffering is a normal part of discipleship?

→ Where do you flee when things get tough?

FOR FURTHER MEDITATION

Read Psalms 34, 52 and 56.

STUDY 6: 1 SAMUEL 23:1 – 26:25

This is a large section but reading the flow of these stories together is a helpful thing to do in a group.

INTRODUCTION: 'THE NO-HOLDS-BARRED' QUESTION

→ *What strikes you as we read this passage through? What stands out as surprising, encouraging or difficult?*

WHAT DOES IT SAY?

→ *In chapter 23 compare the Ziphites with Jonathan. What is their attitude to David?*

→ *Compare David's concerns with Saul's. What is their priority?*

→ *In chapter 24 what reasons does David give for not killing Saul?*

→ *How does Saul respond?*

→ *In chapter 25 what reasons does Abigail give for not killing Nabal?*

→ *How does David respond?*

→ *In chapter 26 what reasons does David give for not killing Saul?*

→ *How does Saul respond?*

WHAT DOES IT MEAN?

→ *How do these stories link?*

→ *What is Abigail's role and significance?*

→ *Why is it important for David to be blameless?*

→ *In what ways is David suffering?*

→ *How do these stories point to Jesus?*

SO WHAT?

→ *How does knowing Jesus is the righteous suffering king affect your life?*

→ *Are you prepared to remind others of God's promises? What makes you hesitate?*

FOR FURTHER MEDITATION

Read Psalms 54 and 57.

STUDY 7: 1 SAMUEL 27:1 – 29:11

INTRODUCTION: 'THE NO-HOLDS-BARRED' QUESTION

→ What strikes you as we read this passage through? What stands out as surprising, encouraging or difficult?

WHAT DOES IT SAY?

→ David and Saul both face a crisis point. What is it and how do they respond to it?

WHAT DOES IT MEAN?

→ Despite having to live with the Philistines, how does David remain guiltless? (See 26:18; 27:8-9; 29:9.)

→ Why is this important?

→ Why does God allow Samuel to speak from the grave? (See Leviticus 19:31; 20:6.) [30]

→ Summarise what these chapters teach us about God's sovereignty.

SO WHAT?

→ How do you understand God's sovereignty?

→ How does your knowledge of God's control affect you in a crisis?

→ When God is against you, what hope is there? (See Psalm 2.)

→ Is Saul's situation any worse than all of us separated from Christ? (See Ephesians 2:12.)

→ Do you really believe that without Christ there is no hope?

→ If you really believed this, in what ways would your life change?

STUDY 8: 1 SAMUEL 30:1 – 31:13

INTRODUCTION: 'THE NO-HOLDS-BARRED' QUESTION

→ What strikes you as we read this passage through? What stands out as surprising, encouraging or difficult?

WHAT DOES IT SAY?

→ List the different adversities that have to be faced here.

→ How does David face each one?

→ How does Saul?

WHAT DOES IT MEAN?

→ What is the difference between Saul and David? (Think about what David knows about God.)

→ Why do we get details about the Egyptian and David's men?

→ Compare chapter 30 with Hannah's prayer of 2:1–10.

→ Why does part one of Samuel end here?

→ What promises have been fulfilled?

SO WHAT?

→ In what ways does the picture of David reveal Jesus to us?

→ Do you really understand Jesus' suffering?

→ Do you really understand Jesus' grace?

→ Do you share the hope of David?

→ Do you share the faith of Hannah?

Notes

INTRODUCTION

1. Jefferson Davis, *John, Meditation and Communion with God* (Illinois: IVP Academic, 2012), p. 20.

CHAPTER 2. IS THERE A 'RIGHT ANSWER'?

2. Barthes, Roland, *The Pleasure of the Text*, translated by Richard Miller (New York: Hill and Wang, 1975), p. 62.

3. Kahneman, Daniel, *Thinking, Fast and Slow* (London: Penguin, 2011).

4. Simons, Daniel, '*The Monkey Business Illusion*' (http://www. youtube.com/watch? v=IGQmdoK_ZfY).

5. Kahneman, Daniel, *Thinking, Fast and Slow*, p. 24.

6. Carson, Don, *Becoming Conversant with the Emerging Church* (Michigan: Zondervan, 2005), p. 119.

7. Ibid., p. 119.

CHAPTER 3. APPROACHING GOD'S WORD

8. David Gordon, T., *Why Johnny Can't Preach* (New Jersey: P&R Publishing, 2009), p. 48.

9. Nietzsche, Friedrich, *Daybreak* (1881), translated by R.J. Hollingdale (Cambridge University Press, 1997), p. 5.

10. Miedema, John, *Slow Reading* (Minnesota: Litwin Books, 2008), p. 63.

11. Fletcher, Lancelot R., *Slow Reading – The affirmation of authorial intent* (http://www.freelance-academy.org/slowread.htm), accessed 19 April 2013.

12. For recommended commentaries try: D.A. Carson, *New Testament Commentary Survey* (Michigan: Baker Academic, 2013); or Dr Tremper Longman III, *Old Testament Commentary Survey* (Michigan: Baker Academic, 2013).

13. Nielson, Kathleen Bushwell, *Bible Study: Following the Ways of the Word* (New Jersey: P&R Publishing, 2012), p. 64.

CHAPTER 4. MODELS OF BIBLE STUDIES

14. David Helm adapts this model for use in one-to-one studies and outlines it in a very helpful way. See David Helm, *One-to-One Bible Reading* (Waterloo, New South Wales: St Matthias Press, 2011), p. 43.

CHAPTER 5. THE 'BIG QUESTION' MODEL

15. This is similar to David Helm's model, which he calls COMA and which stands for Context, Observation, Meaning, Application. See David Helm, *One-to-One Bible Reading*.

CHAPTER 6. MEDITATING ON GOD'S WORD

16. Peterson, Eugene, *Eat This Book* (London: Hodder &

Stoughton, 2006), p. 90.

[17.] Ibid., p. 91.

[18.] Keller, Tim, *The Reason for God* (London: Hodder & Stoughton, 2008), p. 114.

[19.] Schaeffer Macaulay, *Susan, For the Children's Sake* (Illinois: Crossway, 1984), p. 104.

CHAPTER 7. NUTS AND BOLTS

[20.] There is a debate as to the meaning of Tyndale's statement and it is used by some to advocate dynamic equivalent and colloquial translations of the Bible. I agree with Leland Ryken that this is to misunderstand Tyndale. See http://community.beliefnet.com/translating_gods_word/blog/2012/06/11/william_tyndales_plowboy_reconsidered

[21.] http://www.thereader.org.uk/

[22.] Suggested books for exploring this subject further are: Claire Smith, *God's Good Design* (Waterloo, New South Wales: Matthias Media, 2012); Carrie Sandom, *Different by Design* (Fearn, Scotland: Christian Focus, 2012); and Kathy Keller, *Jesus, Justice and Gender Roles* (Michigan: Zondervan, 2014).

[23.] http://www.desiringgod.org/blog/posts/wimpy-theology-and-true-womanhood

APPENDIX 1.

FIVE 'BIG QUESTION' BIBLE STUDIES IN MARK

[24.] Notes for leaders: the words quoted at Jesus' baptism come from Psalm 2:7 and Isaiah 42:1. This reveals Jesus as God's promised messiah, powerful king and suffering servant.

25. Notes for leaders: the ESV translation shows the repetitions most clearly. The word 'immediately' emphasises Jesus' power and authority as He breaks into the world. The words 'teaching' and 'authority' are particularly highlighted by Mark.

26. Notes for leaders: 1:38 is the first of three mission statements Jesus gives in Mark's gospel to explain why He came. See also Mark 2:17 and 10:45. Jesus prays in Mark's gospel at times of significance: in 3:7 before appointing the twelve; in 6:46 before the disciples recognise Him as the Christ; and in 14:32 before the cross.

27. See Leviticus 13:45–46 and 14:1–9.

28. In 2:25–26 Jesus refers to 1 Samuel 21. It is helpful to introduce this story. Jesus likens Himself to the anointed king in waiting who faced persecution. In the next few verses Jesus is facing those who want to kill Him.

APPENDIX 2.
EIGHT 'BIG QUESTION' BIBLE STUDIES IN 1 SAMUEL

29. Notes for leaders: 'God sees according to his heart, i.e. God's point of view is determined by his own will and purpose', as pointed out by John Woodhouse, *1 Samuel: Looking for a Leader* (Illinois: Crossway, 2008), p. 287.

30. Notes for leaders: God is in control of life and death. See 1 Samuel 2:6 and Mark 9:4.